Train Your Brain

Puzzles

BOOK A

Developing Problem Solving Skills in School Students

The First 'GRADED PUZZLE SERIES'

Train Your Brain

Puzzles

Developing Problem Solving Skills in School Students

The First 'GRADED PUZZLE SERIES'

By

Terry Carter

Supported By

Sanmeen Kaur

ARIHANT PUBLICATIONS (INDIA) LIMITED

arihant

Arihant Publications (India) Limited
All Rights Reserved

卐 © Publisher

No part of this publication may be re-produced, stored in a retrieval system or distributed in any from or by any means, electronic, mechanical, photocopying, recording, scanning, web or otherwise without the written permission of the publisher. Arihant has obtained all the information in this book from the sources believed to be reliable and true. However, Arihant or its editors or authors or illustrators don't take any responsibility for the absolute accuracy of any information published and the damages or loss suffered thereupon.

卐 Administrative & Production Offices

Corporate Office

'Ramchhaya' 4577/15, Agarwal Road, Darya Ganj, New Delhi -110002
Tele: 011- 47630600, 43518550; Fax: 011- 23280316

Head Office

Kalindi, TP Nagar, Meerut (UP) - 250002
Tele: 0121-2401479, 2512970, 4004199; Fax: 0121-2401648
All disputes subject to Meerut (UP) jurisdiction only.

卐 Sales & Support Offices

Agra, Ahmedabad, Bengaluru, Bhubaneswar, Bareilly, Chennai, Delhi, Guwahati, Haldwani, Hyderabad, Jaipur, Jalandhar, Jhansi, Kolkata, Kota, Lucknow, Meerut, Nagpur & Pune

卐 **ISBN :** 978-93-5251-242-3

Typeset by Arihant DTP Unit at Meerut

PRODUCTION TEAM

Publishing Manager : Amit Verma

Project Manager	Karishma Yadav	Cover Design	Darin Zaidi
Project Coordinator	Divya Gusain	Layout & Design	Shanu Mansoori
Project Reader	Reena Garg	Type Setting	Vinay Sharma

For further information about the products from Arihant,
log on to www.arihantbooks.com *or email to* info@arihantbooks.com

Train Your Brain

Puzzles

BOOK A

Developing Problem Solving Skills in School Students

The First 'GRADED PUZZLE SERIES'

CONTENTS

Let's Start to TRAIN THE BRAIN

'Train Your Brain' Puzzles Book A contains different types of puzzles; Picture Puzzles, Math Puzzles, Word Puzzles, Logic Puzzles etc that will make you think logically. We assure that you will find your mind more streamlined, stretched & logical by the end of this book. Book A of this series has been especially prepared for school students to sharpen their thinking skills and problem solving skills.

Through this book, we will be testing all the dimensions of your logical thinking abilities. The puzzles given here range from downright easy to essentially impossible. All the puzzles given in this book involve explicit or implicitly clearly defined procedures for solving them. Wherever required we have provided illustrations to help you understand the puzzle perfectly clear and understandable.

Although we have given the solutions at the end of the book but we advice you to 'Take the Challenge' and See! If you can figure out the puzzles before you look up the given explanation.

So push the boundaries of your thinking ahead and have fun solving these puzzles, one thing for sure-you will never be bored while solving these puzzles.

UNRAVEL THE MYSTERY

How to solve? There are many defined and undefined ways to solve a puzzle. The most sorted one is to have a list of facts that describe the information provided in the puzzles.

SOLVING LOGICAL PUZZLES

Step 1 **Analyzing the Puzzle** Always read the puzzles and clues given in it.

Step 2 **Arrangement of Information** Use the grid (table) as you find a information.

Step 3 **Compiling the Information** Read through the clues one at a time filling in what you discover as you go.

Step 4 **Extracting the Information** Look at the grid to discover what you can figure out now.

Step 5 **If still It Is Required** Review the puzzle and find clues, is there is still an unknown.

SOLVING MATHEMATICAL PUZZLES

Step 1 **Find and Use a Pattern** Identify a pattern, and then extend that pattern to solve the problem.

Step 2 **Build a Model** Use objects to represent the situation and the possible solutions.

Step 3 **Draw a Picture or Diagram** Show what is happening in the problem with a picture or a diagram.

Step 4 **Make a Table and/or a Graph** Organise and record your data in a table, chart, or graph. You are more likely to find a pattern or see a relationship when it is shown visually.

Step 5 **Write a Mathematical Sentence** If the problem involves numbers and number operations, a mathematical sentence or expression of a relationship with numbers or symbols, can help make the solution clearer.

Step 6 **Use Guess and Check, or Trial and Error** Even if a potential solution does not work, it may give you clues to other possibilities or help you to better understand the problem.

Step 7 **Break the Problem into Parts** If a problem is too large or complicated simplify it by breaking the problem into smaller and more manageable parts.

Step 8 **Work Backwards** Considering the goal first can make some problems easier. It helps you develop a strategy that leads to the solution by backing through the process.

Step 9 **Change Your Point of View** When a strategy is not working, discard what you are doing and try something else. This may help you think about the problem in a different way.

Puzzles

1.

At Bombay Stock Exchange, traders in order to code the prices of articles/commodities in the trading sessions, used the letters of 'PSICHOLAZY' in the form of 0 to 9, respectively.

What will be the code for the commodity whose price currently stands at ₹ 875.50?

2.

Four small kindergarten students were given the task of making a collection of letters that will look same in the mirror. All the four boys completed their task.

Which of the boys has made the proper collection of letters that would look the same in the mirror?

Boy 1 : O S M I H O M

Boy 2 : V H R T R V H

Boy 3 : H I M O S T A

Boy 4 : A O V I V O A

3.

In the birthday party of my daughter Aslesha, there were 30 people, there are thrice as many women as men and twice as many children as men.

How many of each are there available in this party?

4.

Four girls are sitting on a bench to be photographed facing towards North. Shikha is to the left of Reena. Manju is to the right of Reena. Rita is between Reena and Manju.

Who would be second from the left in the photograph?

(a) Reena

(b) Shikha

(c) Manju

(d) Rita

5.

Each alphabet points to a row of six numbers. Which row is the odd one out?

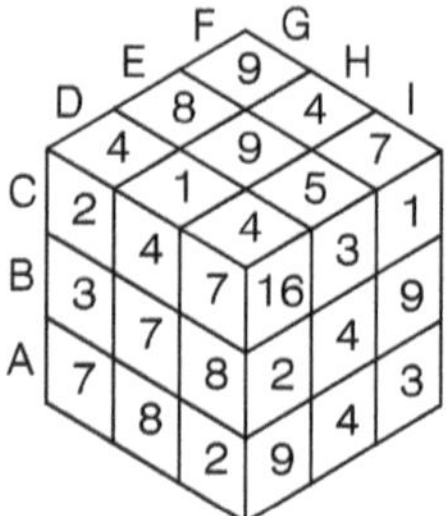

6.

A man caught a fish. It weighted $\frac{5}{7}$ kg + $\frac{5}{7}$ of its own weight.

What is its original weight?

7.

The mathematical signs connecting the numbers below have been left out but have been supplied on four tiles given below. Your job is to place the tiles between the numbers, so that the final answer is 3. All operations are done in a left to right order.

5 □ 2 □ 3 □ 5 □ 4 = 3

[+] [−] [×] [÷]

8.

Rohan Mehra was given the task of assigning numbers to the letters. The letters L, M, N, O, P, Q, R, S and T in their order are to be substituted by nine integers 1 to 9, value of T being the greatest. 4 is assigned to P. The difference between P and T is 5. The difference between N and T is 3.

Can you help Rohan Mehra to find out, which integer should be assigned to N?

9.

What are the values of a, b, c and d so, that the given number pyramid will be logically correct?

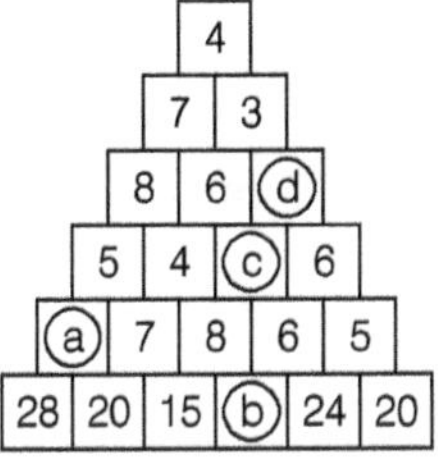

10.

Few boys were playing rugby during the winter. Suddenly, a boy kicked the ball and it went into someone's house. The person in the house liked the quality of the ball and tried to steal it by mixing it with other rugby balls. But the boy to whom this ball belonged knew the identification mark of his ball. The house owner brings 4 rugby balls in front of him and asked the boy to take his own ball from them.

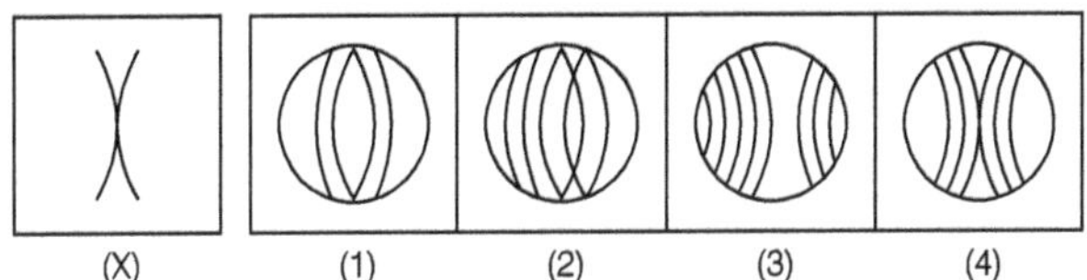

Can you help the boy in finding his original rugby ball, if the identification mark is shown as in figure (X)?

11.

Last year when Imran was in Brazil, while driving the car he saw an another car, which was the victim of an auto theft. So, he noted down the number of that car in the same manner as he saw in the side window mirror. He gave the policeman the following number and he was able to catch the thief.

Can you tell the number of the car, if the number given by Imran to the policeman was ᗺЯI⅃Ƨ9٢∂Ƨ?

12.

Designer Piotr made these glass mirrors for the games room in a client's house. The client, Joshua, is a video-game maker with a playful character and when he asked Piotr to rehang the mirrors he left his instructions in the form of a sequence of clues. Can you help Piotr work out the new sequence from these clues?

Clues:

1. The white shapes are now adjacent.
2. The star has moved one place.
3. The square is now between the circle and the star.

13.

You are trying to fill your bathtub with both hot and cold water, but you accidentally forgot to put the stopper in the drain. The hot tap takes 4.5 min to fill the bathtub. The cold tap takes 12 min to fill the bathtub. The plug hole takes 18 min to empty a full bathtub.

How long will it take to fill the bathtub completely?

14.

Raag Deepak invented by Tansen consists of exactly six notes sa, re, ga, ma, pa and ni. Tansen used the notes from the lowest (the first note of the scale) to the highest (the sixth note of the scale). Each note appears once and only once in the scale. The interval between the notes are all equal.

The following is the information for Tansen notes :

I. 'pa' is lower than 'ni'.

II. 're' is higher than 'sa'.

III. 'ma' is somewhere between 'sa' and 're'.

IV. There is no note between 'ga' and 're'.

Can you determine the lowest note sung by Tansen?

15.

Sachin starts from his house and walks Westward. He, then takes a left turn and then a right, before each turn he walks 3 km. In which direction is he walking now in respect to the starting point?

(a) North-East (b) South-West

(c) West (d) East

16.

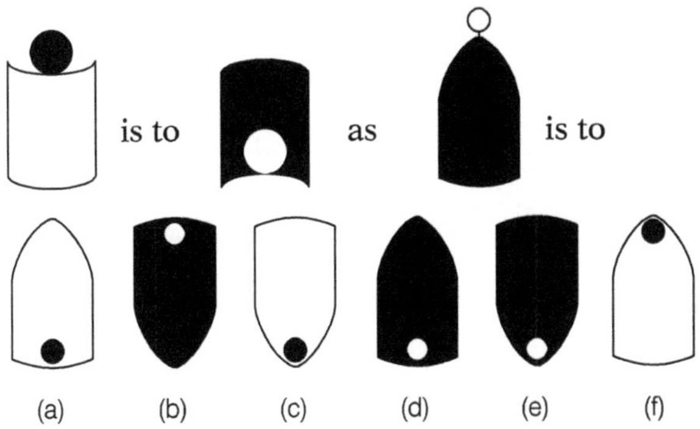

17.

Two people meet at a 'crazy mob' party. One of them asked other to guess his name's from the list of given letters on the basis of some clues.

My name starts from the letter which is second to the right of the letter immediately to the left of the letter which is third to the right of the letter C.

A B C D E F G H

18.

The following words are in a logical progression:

PAINT

UMPIRE

FANATIC

DARKNESS

Which word comes next?

ABDICATED, TRUCULENT, GARDENING, ARILLODE THROUGHOUT, CHIEFTAIN,

19.

Which is the odd one out?

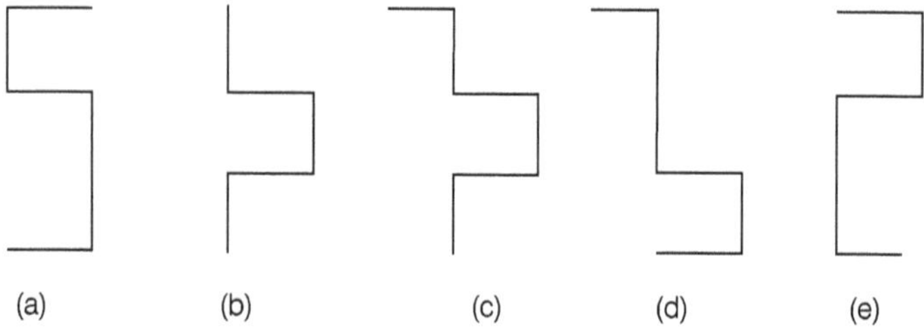

20.

FINAL (FLIRT) ENTER

Using the same logic as in the example above, what word is coded to appear in the bracket below?

BIKER (_ _ _ _ _) RIFLE

(a) BRICK (b) BRILE

(c) BRIEF (d) None of these

21.

US Navy has added a Naval warship in its fleet. The enemy of US has sent some spy disguised in attire of fisherman who were trying to get the details of the ship. The spy were able to see the water image of the number written on the ship.

What was the actual number of the ship, if they saw the following water image?

ՈƧ∂ƖϬ4WƧM3

22.

A square sheet of paper is folded as shown by the dotted lines and then a cut on the corner is made. Which option suggests its look when it is unfolded?

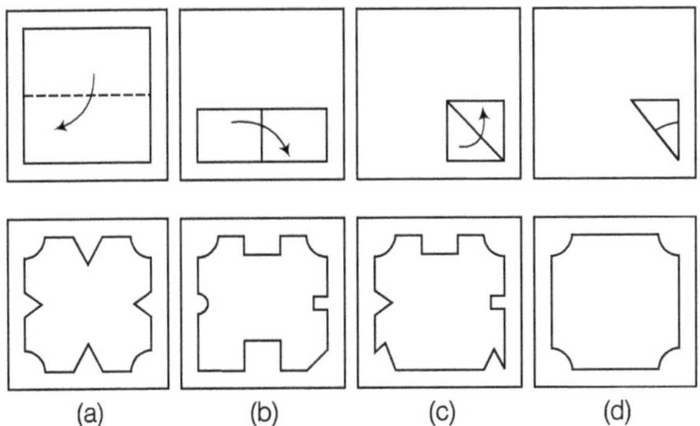

23.

The diagram alongside is made of eight squares, all of the same size. If the perimeter of (distance around) any one of the squares is 100 inch, then what will be the perimeter of the entire shape in inch?

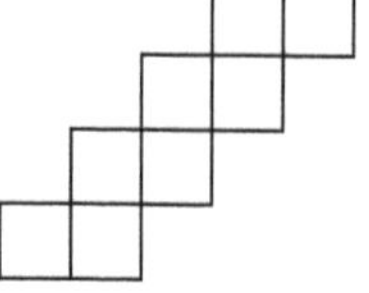

24.

What number should replace the question mark?

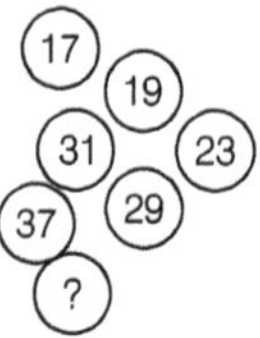

25.

IAEA (International Atomic Energy Agency) has the information that South Korea is developing a hidden nuclear plant. So, the agency sent some special spy to find out the nuclear plant at night. While searching they saw a water image in the river flowing nearby.

How the water image looked like, if they able to see NUCLEAR in actual sense?

26.

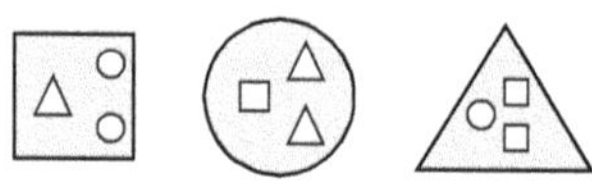

Can you find the shape that would continue the series above?

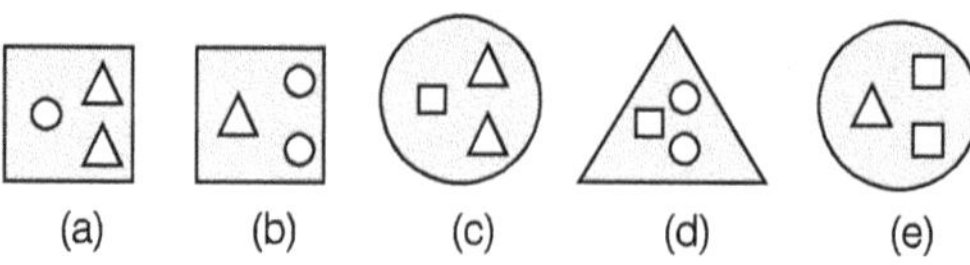

27.

There are many rash drivers in Delhi. Last week when I was driving my car I saw a car, which was running at very high speed and had hit an old man two kilometre before. That car ranaway by overtaking my car and I tried to note down the number of the car, but could see the number of the car in the mirror of my car, which seemed very obstinate.

Can you help me determine the image I saw in the mirror, if the car had the following number?

DL9CG4728

(a) ᗡ⅃୧ƆӘᔨ٦Ƨ8 (b) 8Ƨ٢ᔨӘƆ୧Γᗡ

(c) 8Ƨ٦ᔨӘƆ୧⅃ᗡ (d) 8Ƨ٢ᔨӘƆ୧⅃ᗡ

28.

I was playing with my small children and my wife was standing at MAHO beach. Suddenly, I saw a plane flying over MAHO beach having some number plate on it. I was able to see the water image of the plane.

Can you determine the plane's number, if water image of the plane's number is ΛⱯ⅄Ո8Ⴕ3୧?

29.

You have picked 667 apples from the trees in your orchard, which you are putting into bags to give to your neighbours. You wish to put an equal number of apples into each bag and you wish to use as few bags as possible. How many apples should you put into how many bags?

30.

From the boarding school, three sisters travel home on different days of the month and come back the same day. One travels every 5 days, one travels every 6 days and one travels every 7 days. When will they all return to the school at the same time?

31.

Al beats Bill at chess but loses to Hillary. Chelsea usually wins against Bill but never against Hillary. Who is the weakest player?

32.

What comes next in the sequence?

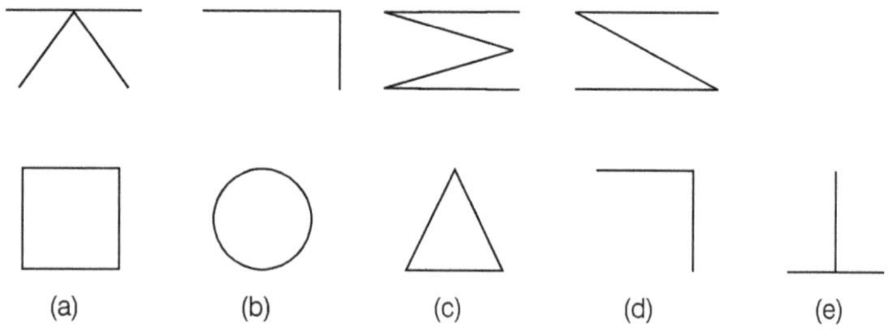

33.

There are several intelligent Zoologist in Science College, Patna. During the class, one of the professors made the statements, 'If the animal which can walk are called 'swimmers', animals who crawl are called 'flying'. Those who living in water are called 'snakes' and those which fly in the sky are called 'hunters', then what will a lizard be called?

34.

Three kinds of apples are mixed in a box. How many apples must you take to be sure of at least 2 apples of one kind and atleast 3 apples of one kind?

35.

If  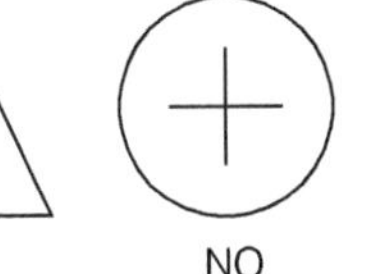 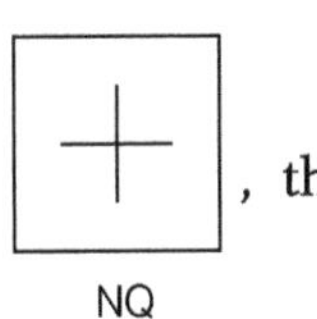 , then

LM NO LP NQ

what is ?

36.

The TRAI (Telecom Regulatory Authority of India) has made it compulsory for the mobile company to bring their product with IMEI number for better tracking and management of phone theft. A mobile company launched its mobile with the following IMEI number.

1st mobile	2nd mobile	3rd mobile	4th mobile	5th mobile	6th mobile
J 2 Z	K 4 X	L 7 V	?	N 16 R	O 22 P

Can you determine the 4th IMEI number on the phone?

37.

My daughter Aslesha is a very intelligent child. She speaks certain English alphabet and asks me to tell the letters which she missed in between.

Can you tell me which letters she missed, if she spoke like this?

adb_ac_da_cddcb_dbc_cbda

38.

In an Art and Crafts class, the teacher Mrs. Carter gave a task of resembling the unfolded form of figure (Z) to the four students.

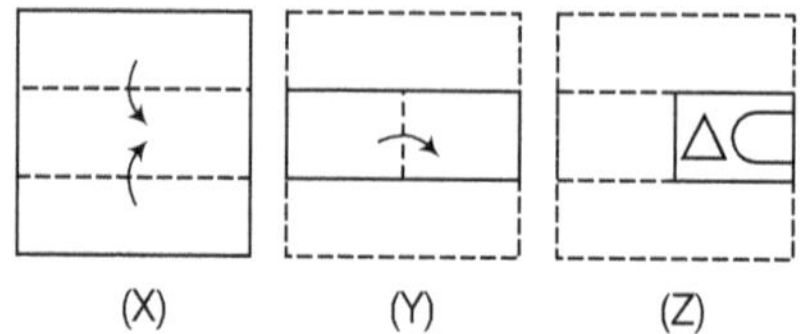

All the four students completed their task. Can you determine which of the students has resemble the correct unfolded form of figure (Z)?

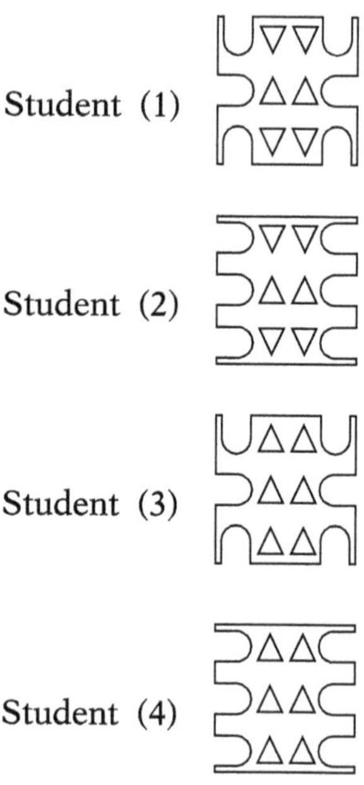

39.

What number should replace the question mark (?) to follow a definite rule?

$14 + 55 \rightarrow 69$

$28 + 23 \rightarrow 60$

$22 + 31 \rightarrow 35$

$17 + 28 \rightarrow 99$

$41 + 27 \rightarrow ?$

40.

If &*+ # is to +#&*

Then, +>#= is to ?

(a) =>+#

(b) #=+>

(c) #+>=

(d) =>+#

41.

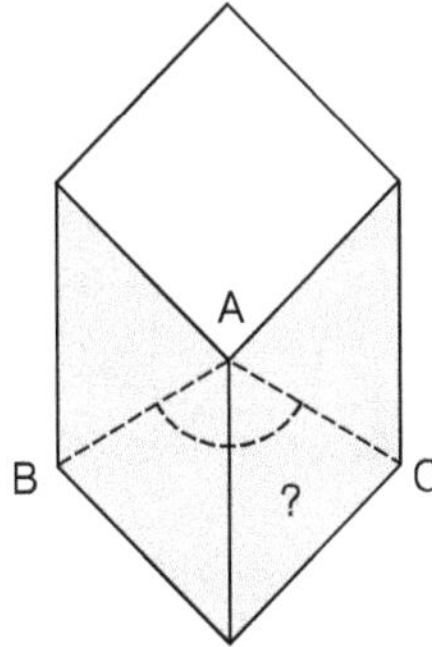

Two diagonals have been drawn on two faces of the cube. Using the logical reasoning and lateral thinking, can you work out the angle between the two diagonals AB and AC?

42.

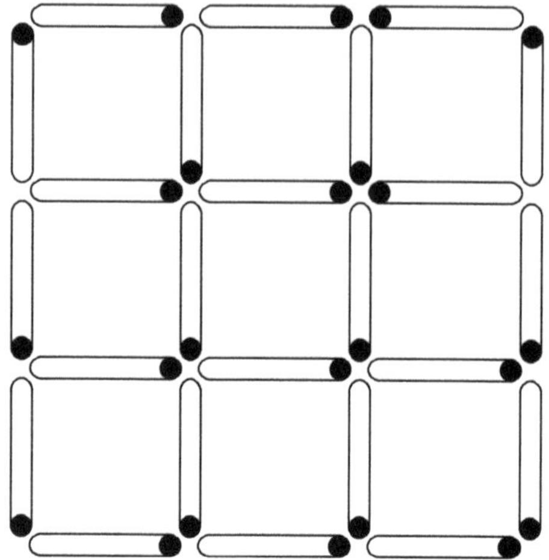

Here is an ice cream stick puzzle that will put you in a good humour, if you can figure out the solution. We have arranged 24 sticks so that they form nine squares. Can you remove four of these sticks so that we are left with just five squares?

43.

What comes next in the sequence?

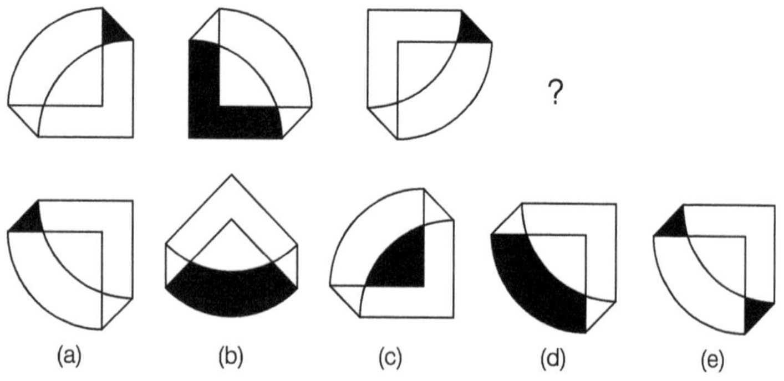

44.

What four digits should appear in the middle section?

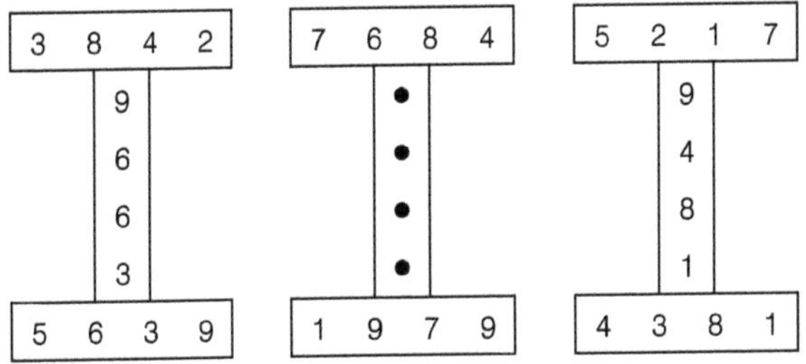

45.

On a google map I checked out the distance from my house to certain cities and to my amazement the distances of these cities followed a specific pattern which is given below:

BERLIN– 200 miles

PARIS– 300 miles

ROME– 400 miles

AMSTERDAM– 300 miles

According to above pattern, can you find out the distance of 'CARDIFF' city from my house?

46.

In a puzzle game played by the family cousins Ramita said, "Romi has a brother Anil, Romi is the son of Chandra and Bimal is Chandra's father." In term of relationship, what is Anil of Bimal?

(a) Son (b) Grandson

(c) Brother (d) Grandfather

47.

What number should replace the question mark?

2836 : 13

9423 : 14

7229 : ?

48.

One day I came out from my house and I saw three ants are sitting at the three corners of a path in form of an equilateral triangle. Each ant starts randomly, picks a direction and starts to move along the edge of the triangle. Can you determine the probability that none of the ants collide?

49.

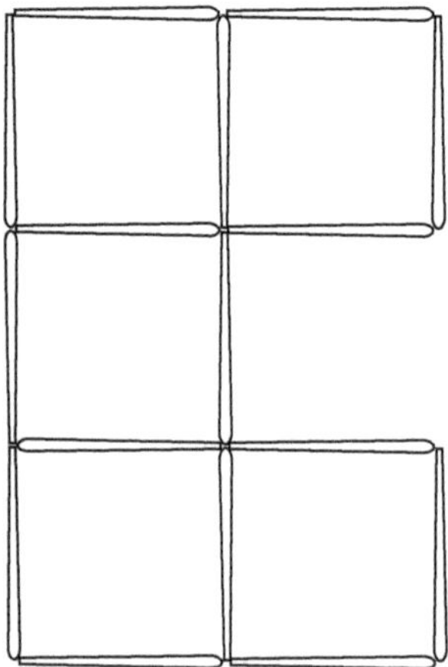

Here is an interesting little puzzle that should keep you busy for a few minutes... or more. Above are five squares constructed from sixteen toothpicks. Your job is to move three of these toothpicks to new positions, so that we now have four equal squares.

50.

Agatha was going to buy eight books, but it turned out she was ₹ 7 short. What she did was buy just seven books and was left with ₹ 5 to spare. How much did a single book cost, if all the titles she was interested in cost the same and how much money was she carrying?

51.

As they say, beggars can't be choosers, in fact beggar take what they can get. A beggar on the street can make one cigarette out of every 6 cigarette butts he finds. After one whole day of searching and checking public ashtrays the beggar finds a total of 72 cigarette butts. How many cigarettes can he make (also smoke) from the butts he finds?

52.

Mr. Booshi had an urgent meeting at a new venue. He could not find the way to the venue so asked one of the passerby to guide him. The passerby said, ''walk 2 km Northward and take a left turn, walk 5 km and then turn right, walk 3 km and again turn right walk 5 km.'' In which direction was the venue from the point, where Mr. Booshi met the passerby?

53.

Rajan while showing his family trip album to his friends pointed out to a lady, and said, "She is the daughter of the woman who is the mother of the husband of my mother." Who is the lady to Rajan?

54.

All the given bicycles took part in a race. Something really mired happened! The start and finish times of the bicycles became mathematically linked. If you can discover the link you should be able to decide when bicycle D started.

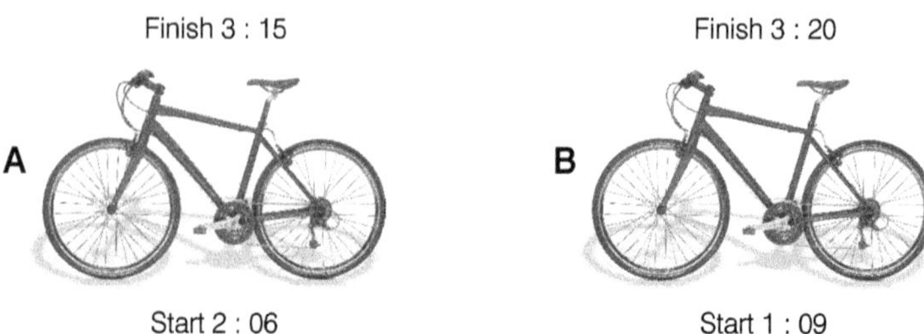

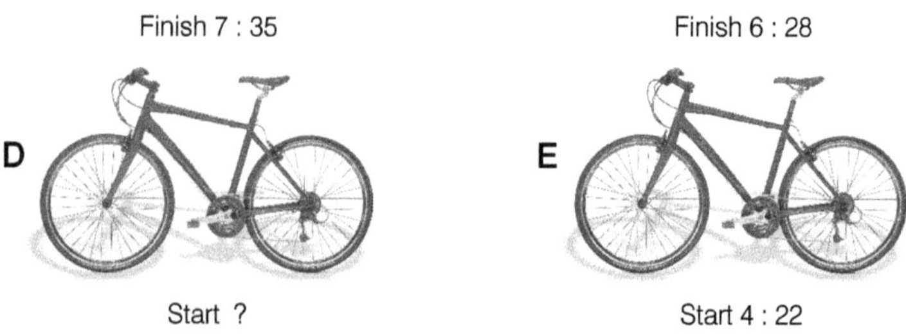

55.

Each horse carries a weight handicap. Can you work out the number of the final horse?

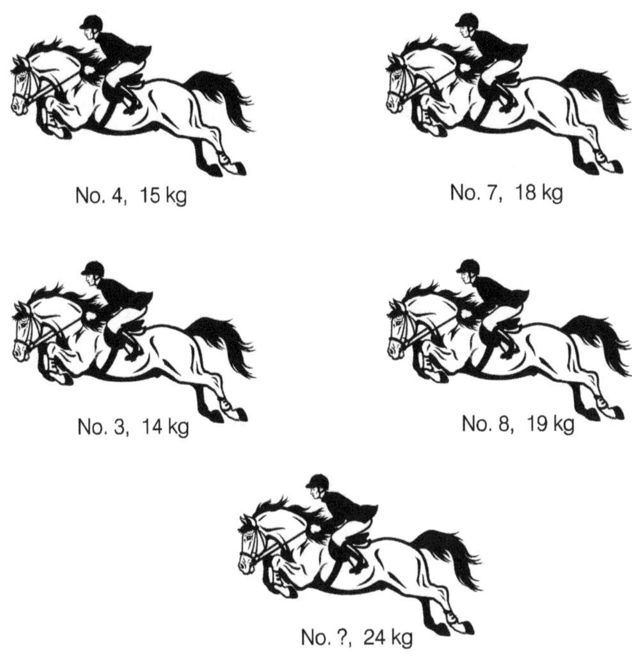

56.

What number should replace the question mark?

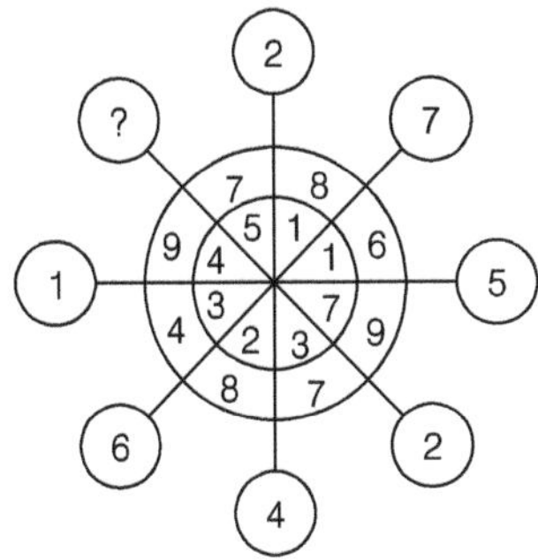

57.

Indian Army was patrolling in the 'Punch sector' of Jammu and Kashmir. Suddenly, Major Subedar Singh shouts 'Ding Dong Dang' which means 'Attacking the Enemy' Sipahi Gheesa Bhagat shouts 'Ping Pong Dong' which means 'Enemy is Retreating'. Captain Bhanu Pratap shouts 'Ding Ping Mong' which means 'Attacking and Retreating'.

Can you tell us the code they used for the 'enemy'?

58.

Based on the following information, find how many pleezorns does Ahmad Adziz have?

Molly O'Brien has 22 pleezorns.

Debbie Reynolds has 28 pleezorns.

Roberto Montgomery has 34 pleezorns.

59.

If I tripled one-quarter of a fraction and multiplied it by that fraction, I would get one-twelfth. What is the original fraction?

60.

A unique type of apple shooting game is played in Spain, where the lover shoots arrow on the apple planted on their girlfriend's head and the marking is done on the basis of the angle with which the arrow hits the apple. According to this game the arrows pattern is as follows. If '→' stands for 'addition', '←' stands for subtraction, '↑' stands for 'division', '↓' stands for 'multiplication,' ' ' stands for 'equal to'.

Determine whether the calculation of the marks done below is correct or not?

$$2 \downarrow 5 \leftarrow 6 \rightarrow 2 \uparrow 6 \quad 1$$

61.

Complete this puzzle by drawing what you think should appear in the empty box.

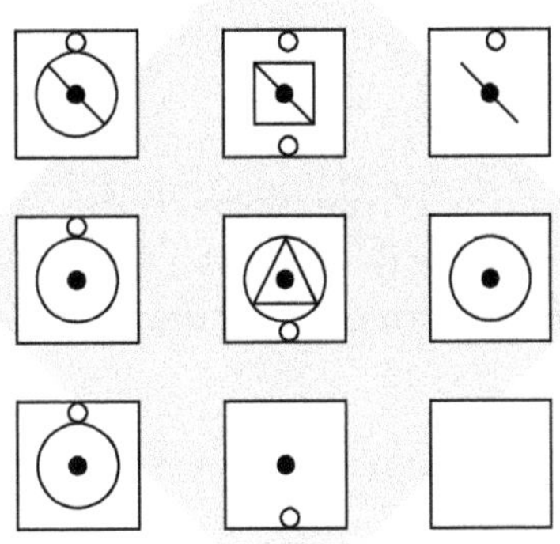

62.

Which day is two days after the day four days before the day immediately following the day two days before Saturday?

Sunday
Monday
Tuesday
Wednesday
Thursday
Friday
Saturday

63.

Arthur and Bert built the brickwork of a house together in 24 days. If Arthur can do only two-thirds as much as Bert, how long would it take each of them working alone?

64.

There are a number of lions and eagles at the zoo. In all, they have 30 heads and 86 legs. How many lions and eagles are there?

65.

I recently returned from a trip. Today is Friday. I returned four days before the day after the day before tomorrow. Find on which day I returned from the trip?

66.

The Municipal Corporation of Delhi has decided to erect a lamppost at two points, so that all roads are lighted at the same time.

Which two points the government should select, if they have following points for the erection of the lamppost?

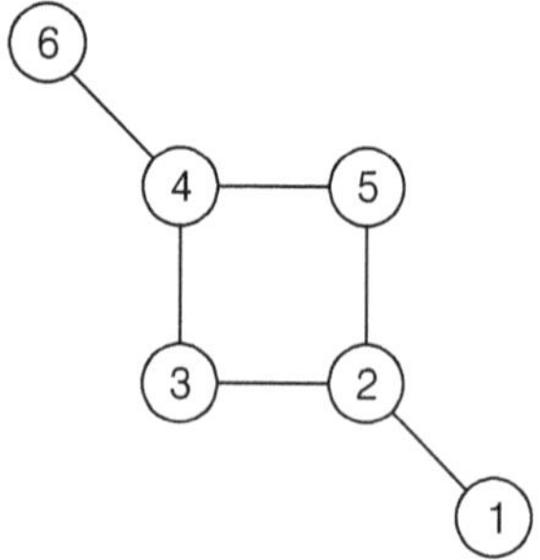

67.

A group of students at a major university was polled to see which courses they were taking. 64% were taking English, 22% were taking a foreign language and 7% were taking both. What percentage of the students polled were taking neither subject?

68.

Here is a cube presented from four different perspectives of the flattened cube given below them. One of the views is incorrect. Can you tell which one?

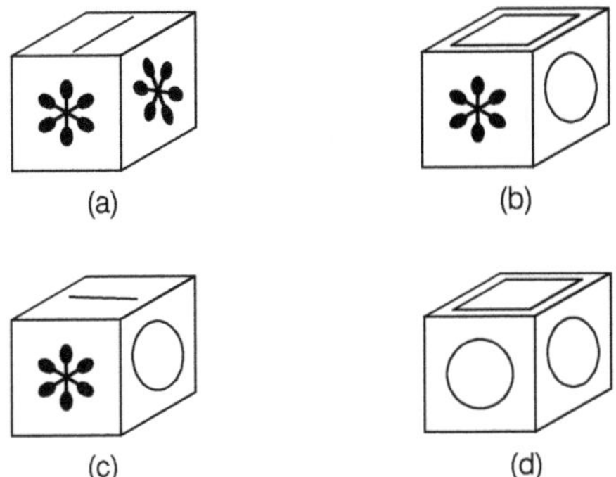

Flattened cube

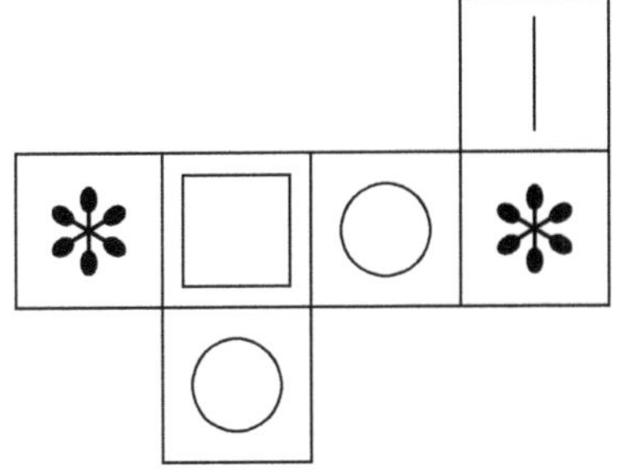

69.

What is this?

Take half of this, and add one to it.

Then triple that, and add on four.

You would have seen a same result, if added 23 to this.

70.

In a magic show, the magician announced to play his magic on the youngest lady amongst the three chosen by him.

If the combined ages of

Alice and Barbara is 76.

Alice and Chloe is 96.

Barbara and Chloe is 140.

Then, on whom did he play his tricks.

71.

These clocks follow a weird kind of logic. What time should the fourth clock face show?

72.

Look at the five drawings. Does (a), (b), (c), (d) or (e) continue the sequence?

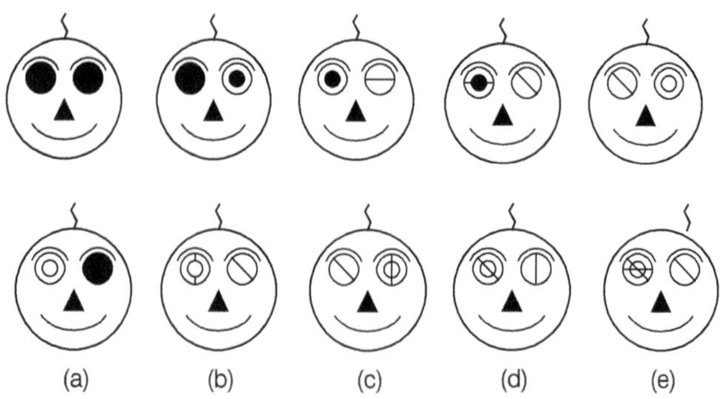

73.

I was having lunch in a South Indian restaurant. The place was crowded. A man excused himself and sat at my table. He began to eat idlis one after the other. As soon as one plate was finished he ordered more. As I sat there discreetly watching him, somewhat stunned, after he finished the last idli he told the waiter that he did not want any more. He took a big gulp of water, looked at me, smiled and said, 'The last one I ate was the 100th idli in the last five days. Each day I ate 6 more than on the previous day. Can you tell me how many I ate yesterday?

74.

Hiram Ballpeene, our local handyman, was hired by Ma Boscomb to replace a section of floor in her attic. He had to cover an opening that was 2 ft wide and 12 ft long. In his truck Hiram had a sheet of plywood that was 3 ft wide and 8 ft long. Being a master carpenter Hiram was able to cut this board into two pieces which covered the hole perfectly. How did he do it?

75.

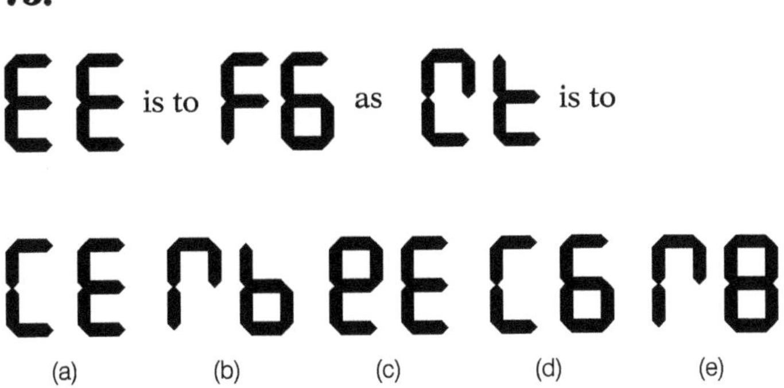

76.

Our group consisted of 400 when we went on an overseas excursion. On our return we were asked, if we had any complaints to make. 240 had no complaints at all. Amongst rest 60 complained about the delays everywhere, 3 complained about the delays, food, and lack of facilities, 11 about food and lack of facilities, 8 about delays and food, and 7 about delays and lack of facilities. An equal number complained about either lack of facilities or food only.

How can you represent these figures on a Venn diagram and calculate the number of persons who complained about the food only?

77.

I was offered a ticket from International Olympic Foundation to watch the game. There were four playgrounds on which four games were being played. Suddenly, I found a mark on my ticket and decided to watch the same game to which this mark belonged. Ticket mark is shown as below in figure (X).

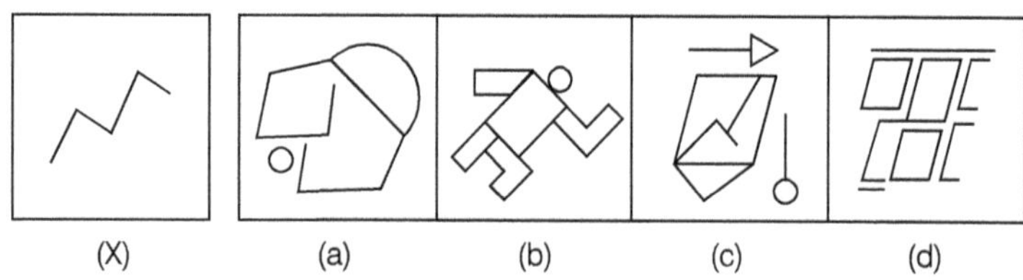

Can you help me find out the game to which this mark belonged to out of the four games shown above?

78.

What number should replace the question mark?

79.

On a certain island, the rainfall follows a very reliable pattern. If it rains in the morning, it is clear in the afternoon. One family comes to the island for their vacation. When they leave. There are 12 clear mornings and 13 clear afternoons. How long was their vacation if it rained for 15 days?

80.

Recently, a flower show was conducted at Mughal Garden where four unique flowers from Amazon was brought in the show. Suddenly, I found a petal of a flower lying on the ground, as shown in the figure (X), so I decided to find the original flower to which this petal belonged.

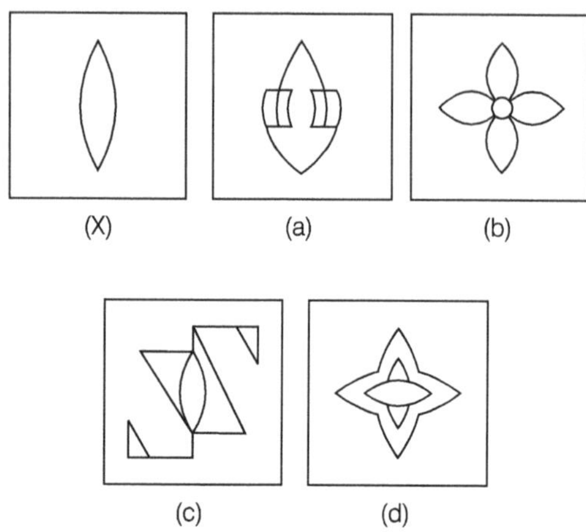

Can you help me in finding the original Amazon flower?

81.

Which is the odd one out?

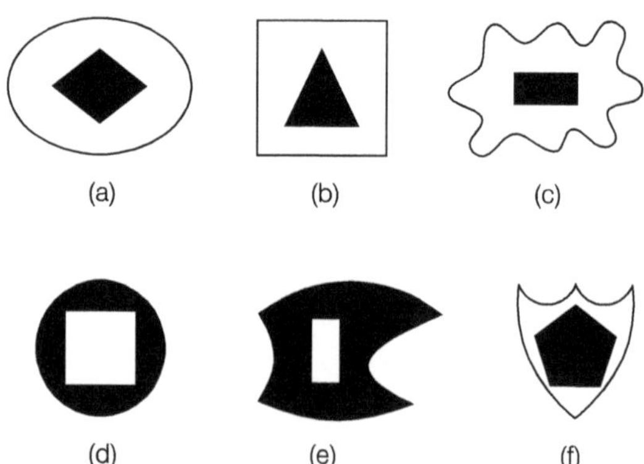

82.

There were 4 students who qualified for the final round of maths Olympiad, they were provided with one question based on circles in which they were asked to follow certain rule that was "As the circle decreases in size, its sectors increases in number".

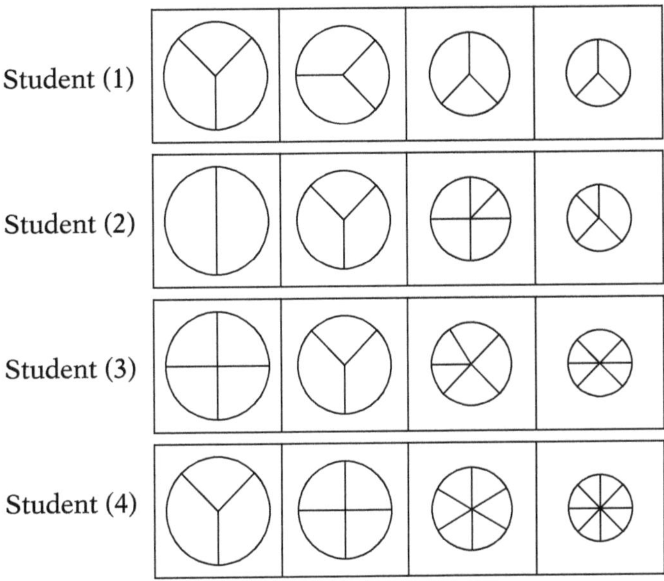

Can you determine which student solved the puzzle correctly?

83.

In a Mathematics class, Mr. White asked his students to be less dependant on calculators and use their skill to solve a problem given below.

If 7^{33} is divided by 10, what will the remainder be? You may get the wrong answer, if you try to solve this on some calculators.

Can you tell correct answer without using a calculator?

84.

Here is a puzzle construction made using Tinkertoy rods and connectors. The construction is made up of nine equal sized triangles. The task is to remove five of these rods in such a way that you will be left with five equal triangles.

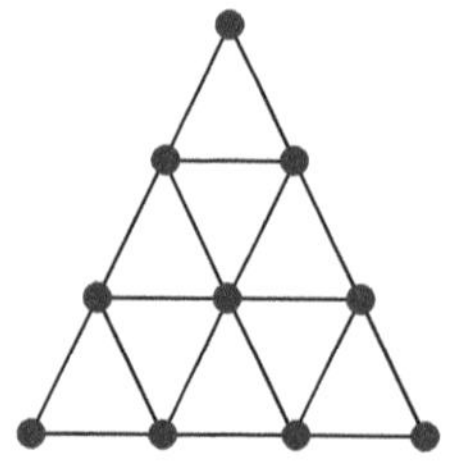

85.

In a game with 24 players that lasts for exactly 50 min, there are 24 players plus 8 reserves who alternate equally with each player. This means that all the players, including reserves, are on the field for the same length of time. How long is that?

86.

In the morning, a news vendor sold two copies of one magazine and five copies of a newspaper for a total of ₹ 15. In the afternoon, he sold five copies of the same magazine and two copies of the same newspaper for a total of ₹ 18.60. What is the cost of one newspaper and one magazine?

87.

Long ago, a young Chinese prince wanted to marry a Mandarin's daughter. The Mandarin decided to test the prince. He gave the prince two empty, porcelain vases, 100 white pearls, and 100 black pearls. "You must put all the pearls in the vases", he told the prince. "After this, I will call my daughter from the room next door. She will take a random pearl from one of the two vases. If this pearl is a black one, you are allowed to marry my daughter." What was the best in which the prince could divide the pearls over the vases?

88.

St. Xavier school organised an annual function in the year 2015. In that annual function, 504 children participated. The ratio of the number of girls to the number of boys is 5 : 3, respectively.

Out of the total girls, 20% participated in dance and the remaining girls participated in solo song, group song and drama in the ratio of 2 : 3 : 4. Two-thirds of the total boys participated in group song and the remaining boys participated in dance and solo song in the ratio of 4 : 5. The principal of the school wanted to know the total number of girls who have participated in group song and drama together. Can you determine the required number of girls?

89.

There are 100 members of the Donald eaters club. Only 15 of them have tried both cauliflower and spinach. Altogether, 72 of them have never tried cauliflower and 81 have never tried spinach.

How many members of the Donald eaters club have never tried cauliflower or spinach?

90.

In the month of November, the Cyclonic Waves hit the coastal areas of America. The Meteorological Department over there issued four wave patterns for the public regarding the original pattern of air movement.

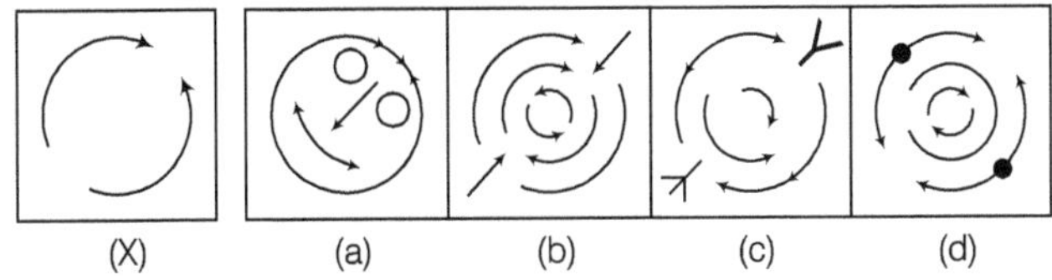

Can you determine the wave pattern the cyclonic wave belonged?

91.

Mrs. Pepper taught her class the basics of squares and cubes of a number. She then gave a question to practice and asked the students to pick the odd one out on the basis of the lecture. The question is as follows

Which would be the correct answer to her question?

92.

Which is the odd one out?

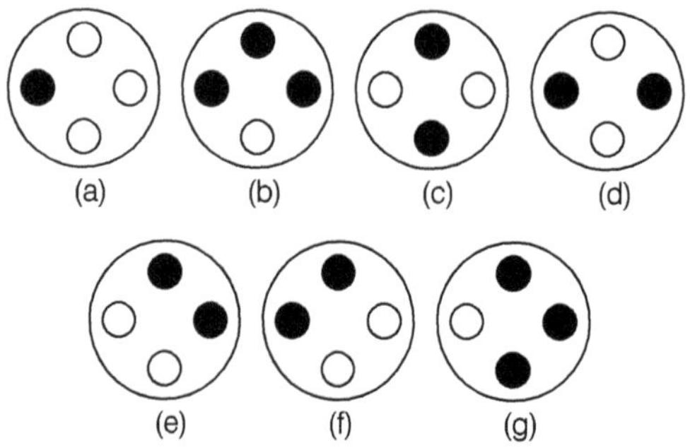

93.

Below are six rays. Choosing two of the rays, how many angles of less than 90° can you form? ($\angle ACB$ is less than 90°).

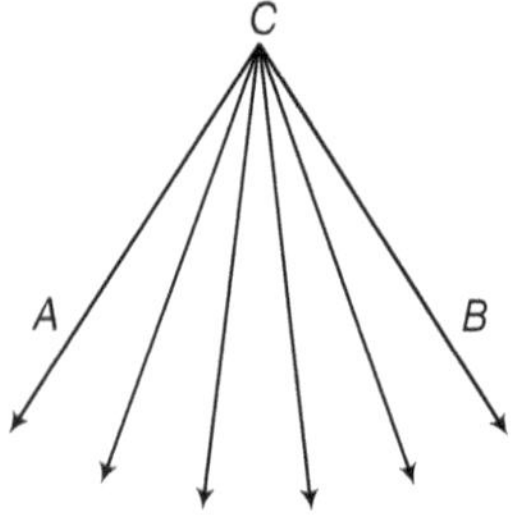

94.

Which two cubes from (a) to (f) cannot be made from the flattened cube?

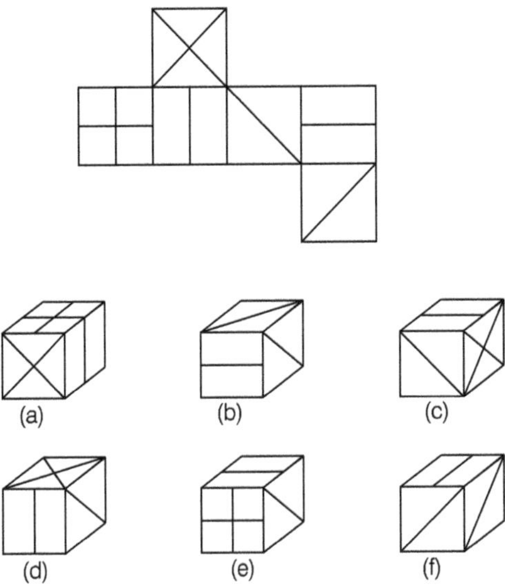

95.

Mr. Benrick forgot his suitcase code and asked his wife to help him crack the code. His witty wife gave him some options and asked him to find the odd one out which is the required code.

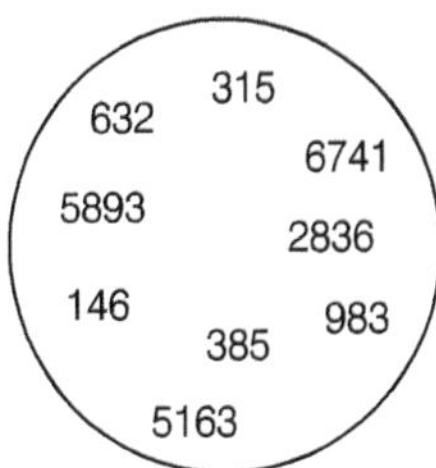

Can you try to find out the required code of the suitcase?

96.

On the Eve of Deepawali, my mother was making some holy pictures. Being a small child my son enquired from her grandma that what is she making to which she replied, I am making some holy symbols and asked my son by drawing 'Swastik' on one side as shown in the figure (X) to find Swastik in the four holy symbols drawn by her.

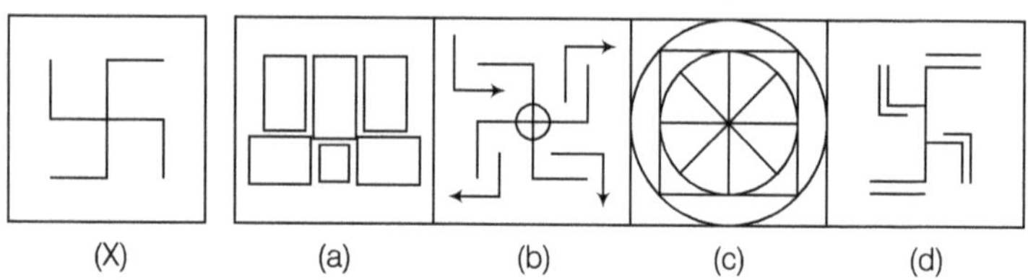

(X) (a) (b) (c) (d)

Can you help my small son to find the 'Swastik' in the four holy symbols?

97.

In a Mathematics class, Mr. Banerjee took a surprise test on rational numbers to check whether the students are able to understand the topic.

What fraction will produce this recurring decimal?

0. 7128888888888...

Can you tell the correct answer for it?

98.

What number should replace the question mark?

99.

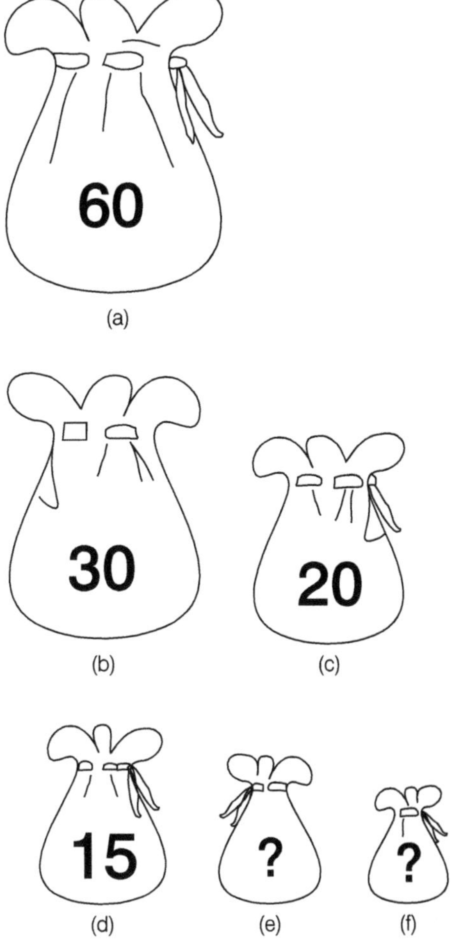

Diver Duncan hit the jackpot and got 6 bags of gold coins. The first four bags contained 60, 30, 20 and 15 gold coins, respectively. After he counted the coins in the remaining two bags he noted that the number of coins in each of the six bags corresponded to a specific progression. Knowing this, can you figure out how many coins were in bags (e) and (f)?

100.

I have an alarm clock placed near my mirror. One day when the alarm rang, I woke up and saw the time, not in the clock, but in the mirror. It was showing the time 7 : 10 early morning, so I woke up and went to the office, but when I reached there it was still 7 : 10.

Can you tell me what time it actually was when I saw the time 7 : 10 in the morning?

101.

Arihant Publication is one such reputed name in the field of various exams. The publication wants to launch five new books on various exams like CAT, MAT, CDS, UPSC and Bank PO.

These five books have to go through proofreading in 6 hours where 1 hour needs to be given to read a book. A lunch break session of 1 hour has to be taken in the third or fourth working hour.

Proofreading cannot be started with CAT's book and has to end in CDS's book. UPSC's book has to follow MAT's book immediately with no break in between.

CAT's book cannot be done immediately after UPSC's book. CAT's book has to precede Bank PO's book immediately with no break in between. A new employee is recruited by Arihant Publication for this purpose. Can you tell him which hour is the lunch break session?

102.

Sid is one and a half times as old as Alf who is one and a half times as old as Jim. Their combined ages total 133. How old are the three men?

103.

A man left a sum of money to his three children. Albert is to get 20% more than Jasper and 25% more than Cyril. Jasper's share is ₹ 3600. How much does Cyril get?

104.

A mathematician will stated that his wife should get one-third of his estate, his son one-fifth, his elder daughter one-sixth, and his younger daughter ₹ 9000. Who received more, his elder daughter or his younger daughter?

105.

D. Ramaswamy, was sitting in front of the interview panel of Civil Services. This panel had a unique method of asking question. In the interview panels language, letter R is denoted by N, D by T, I by U, O by I, E by R, T by O, U by D, N by C and C by E, then how will the interview panel speak when they want D. Ramaswamy to 'INTRODUCE' himself?

106.

Eternal student Gabriel is working on the *zig-zag* Hotel puzzle. The guestbooks each have numbers on them and Gabriel is playing around with them. He arranges them as shown and then asks his colleague, Seamus, to rearrange them in a new sequence on the basis of three clues given by Gabriel (below). Can you help Seamus crack the code?

Here are the clues provided by Gabriel: In the new sequence, the middle numbers add up to 5; the 4 is now to the left of but next to the 1; and the number on the far right is bigger than that on the far left.

107.

There are many skills which we associate with visual thinking. Some of these skills may be much more difficult to master than others. e.g. The ability to mentally rotate objects is often harder than we might imagine.

Try this: If you were to assemble these pieces into a circle, what figure would be formed by the inner lines look like?

108.

What comes next in the sequence?

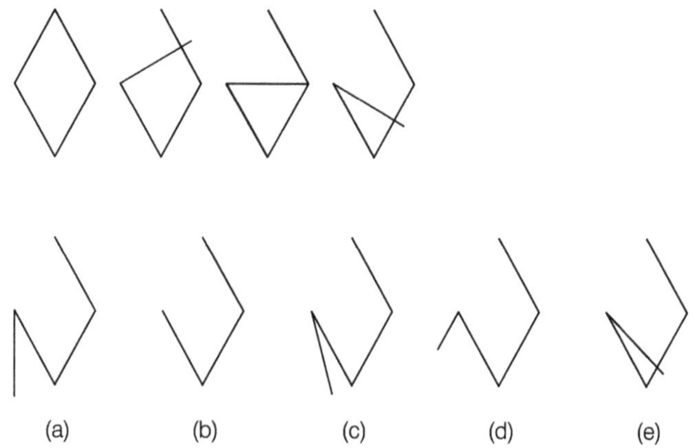

109.

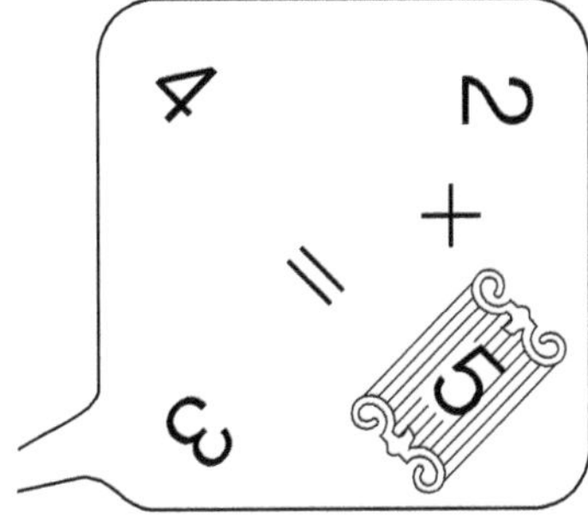

Ruppert, the famous talking rhino, has come up with a new puzzle that should keep you busy for quite a while. Arrange the four numbers 2, 3, 4 and 5, alongwith a plus sign and an equal sign, into a valid mathematical equation.

110.

I am ten years older than my sister. There was a time when I was three times older than she was and in one year I will be twice as old as she is. What is my age now and before how many years ago was my age three times of my sister's age?

111.

Mr. Ezra flyright drew 3 ballons having some figure written in them which are following a specific pattern as given below :

Can you find the missing letters as per the pattern given?

(a) ML (b) QO

(c) KC (d) NP

112.

At a dog show different dogs are numbered as given below:

Corgi– 11

Alsatian– 20

Terrier– 16

Wolfhound– ?

What number should be given to wolfhound?

113.

Last time we were in Paris. Mishka and I fell in love with the Eiffel Tower. She began to insist that we carry the Eiffel tower back to India. I tried to explain to her that such a thing was impossible, but nothing would make her see reason. Finally, I had to promise her that I would have an identical tower made in miniature, for her.

In order to have a smaller replica made I enquired the exact data about the Eiffel Tower. Here, are the details

- The Eiffel Tower is 300 m high.
- It is made of steel.
- The weight of steel used is 8000000 kg.

I have decided to order the model to be made with only 1 kg of steel. How high do you think my Eiffel Tower would be?

114.

While travelling through a train in Jharkhand, my train suddenly stopped in a jungle. After waiting there for long, one of the railway officers told the passengers that Naxalites have bombed four signal system, installed in certain pattern. Out of 15 signals 4 have been destroyed which are as follow:

Z__25 Y B 23 X C__W__19__E 17

Can you find out the code of destroyed railway signals?

115.

I go to the New Delhi Railway Station to receive my uncle, where I see a train schedule chart in which there are two trains A and B.

Both trains have four different types of coaches, *viz*. General, Sleeper, First class and AC.

In train A, there are total 700 passengers. Train B has 30% more passengers than train A.

20% of the passengers of train A are in general coach. One-fourth of the total number of passengers of train A are in AC coach. 23% of passengers of train A are in Sleeper coach. Remaining passengers of train A are in Sleeper coach. The total number of passengers in AC coach in both the trains together is 480. 30% of the number of passengers of train B are in sleeper coach. 10% of the total passengers of train B are in First class coach. The remaining passengers of train B are in General coach. An old man asked me, "What is the total number of passengers in the General coach of train A and the AC coach of train B together?"

116.

Laxmi Vilas Bank is a scheduled private sector bank. To keep its activity of transaction secret the employees of this bank use letters instead of mathematical notation. According to them P denotes '÷', Q denotes '×', R denotes '+' and S denotes '–', then can you tell us what will be the total amount of the transaction (in ₹ lakh), which is required to be calculated at the end of the day, given by the expression below, if the BODMAS rule is followed?

18 Q 12 P 4 R 5 S 6

117.

Is there a number which when divided by 3, gives a remainder 1, when divided by 4, gives a remainder 2, when divided by 5, gives a remainder of 3, and when divided by 6 gives a remainder of 4?

118.

A mathematician from Paglapur was working with Indian Institute of Science, Bengaluru. He had a very unique method of doing the calculations. According to him $>$ denotes '+', $<$ denotes '−', $+$ denotes '÷', $\wedge$ denotes '×', $-$ denotes '=', $\times$ denotes '>' and $=$ denotes '<'.

Can you tell me, which of the following calculations would be true, if he has done the following 4 calculations?

(a) $6 + 3 > 8 = 4 + 2 < 1$

(b) $4 > 6 + 2 \times 32 + 4 < 1$

(c) $8 < 4 + 2 = 6 > 3$

(d) $14 + 7 > 3 = 6 + 3 > 2$

119.

$$\frac{444 - 44}{4} = 100$$

Now, find another way of arranging six 4's to equal 100 just by using any of the mathematical symbols (+, −, ×, ÷) plus brackets and parentheses but no decimals.

120.

Long ago, there was a king who had six sons. The king possessed a huge amount of gold, which he hid carefully in a building consisting of a number of rooms. In each room, there were a number of chests; this number of chests was equal to the number of rooms in the building. Each chest contained a number of gold coins that equaled the number of chests per room. When the king died, one chest was given to the royal barber. The remainder of the coins had to be divided fairly between his six sons.

Is a fair division possible in all situations?

121.

Here is another opportunity to use analytical reasoning, but this puzzle has a slightly different twist.

In a foreign language:

'Kaf navcki roi' means 'Take three pieces.'

'Kir roi palt' means 'Hide three coins.'

'Inoti kaf kir' means 'Cautiously take coins.'

How would you say 'Hide pieces cautiously' in this language?

122.

During a recent trip to Scotland, I filled my petrol tank to the top, a total of 10 gallons. I travelled at 60 mph up the motorway and I knew that I could average 40 miles per gallon. However, the moment I started, my petrol tank developed a leak and four hours later I ground to a halt having run out of petrol. How much petrol had I lost through the leak?

123.

It was vacation time, and so I decided to visit my cousin's home. What a grand time we had! In the mornings, we both would go for a jog. The evenings were spent on the tennis court. Tiring as these activities were, we could manage only one per day, i.e. either we went for a jog or played tennis each day. There were days when we felt lazy and stayed home all day long.

Now, there were 12 mornings when we did nothing, 12 evenings when we stayed at home and a total of 10 days when we jogged or played tennis. For how many days did I stay at my cousin's place?

124.

Each line and symbol which appears in the four outer circles is transferred to the centre circle according to these rules:

If a line or symbol occurs in the outer circles:

once, then it is transferred.

twice, then it is possibly transferred.

three times, then it is transferred.

four times, then it is not transferred.

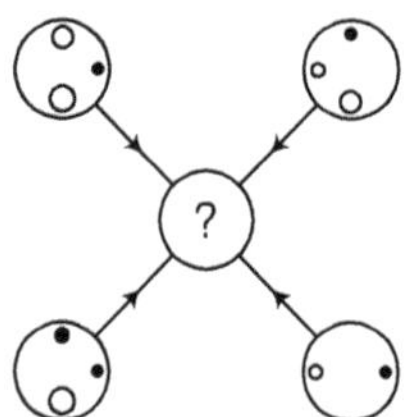

Which of the circles (a), (b), (c), (d) or (e) shown below should appear at the centre of the diagram above?

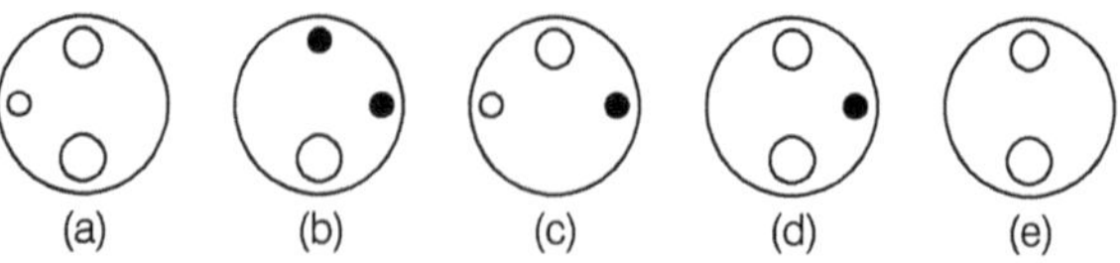

125.

At a holiday camp, there were 38 holiday makers. There will be atleast 19 people who are mutual friends or atleast 19 people who are mutual strangers. True or False?

126.

Five friends live in street corner buildings in New York city. Where should they meet in order to cut down their walking time to a minimum?

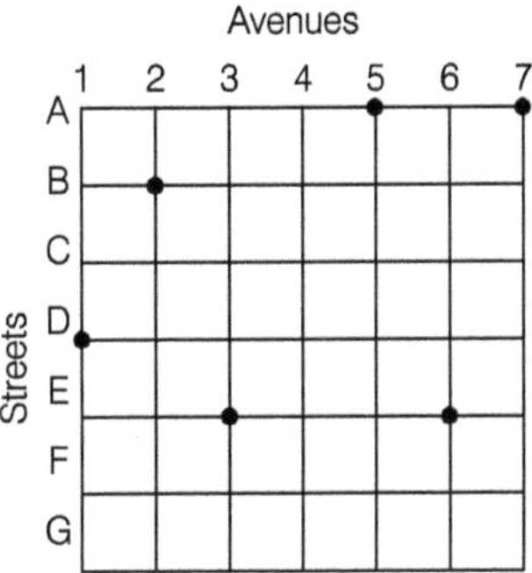

127.

Mr. X granted a land to Mr. Y for some period of time. Due to some miscalculation Mr. X charged Mr. Y some extra amount to which Mr. Y said, "I had a 99 yr lease; $\frac{2}{3}$ of the time past was equal to $\frac{4}{5}$ of the time to come." How much of the lease had expired?

128.

Your Chemistry teacher 'Jenny D' Souza' asks you to convert temperatures from one system of measurement to another. There are new systems for determining temperatures. So, the classic conversions from centigrade, farenheit and Kelvin don't apply.

You are told that 14° in the first system is equal to 36° in the second system. You also know that 133° in the first system is equal to 87° in the second.

What is the method or formula for converting one system to the other? At what temperature will both thermometers read the same?

129.

Anupam travelled from points *A* to *B* (a distance of one mile) at 30 mph. How fast would the car have to travel from points *B* to *C* (also a distance of one mile) to average 60 mph for the entire trip?

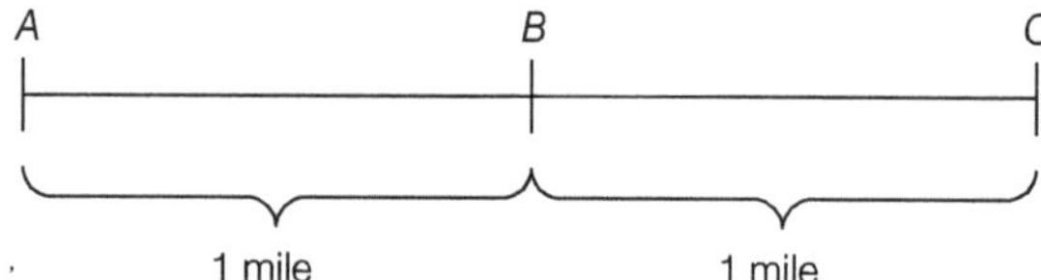

130.

A father and his son take 8 h to dig the entire plot of land. The father working by himself needs 12 h to accomplish the task. How many hours will it take the son to dig the plot by himself?

131.

Ragini starts from her house towards East. After walking a distance of 25 m, she turned towards left and walked 10 m. She then turned right and after moving a distance of 20 m, turned to her right again and walked 20 m. She then turns to the right and walks 7.5 m. Finally, she turns to her right. In which direction is she walking now?

(a) South-East

(b) West

(c) North

(d) North-West

132.

My Dad's friend Mr. Morgan is an Astronomer. One day he invited my family on dinner. After finishing the dinner, we all checked out his study room where I saw a picture on the projector as shown below.

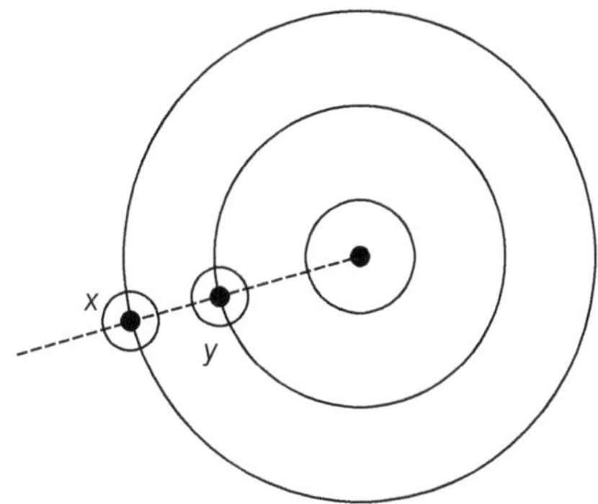

We asked him the concept behind the picture, to which he said that x and y are two satellites. If satellite y takes three years to make one revolution and satellite x takes five years to make one revolution, in how many years will they both be exactly in line as they are now?

133.

Which pentagon should replace the question mark(?) (a), (b), (c) or (d)?

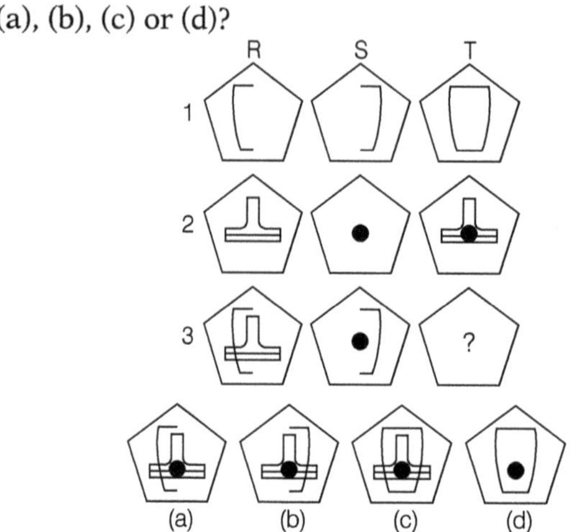

134.

Father Gonsalvez has a very unique Christmas Tree which keeps the count of number of visitors in the church on the eve of Christmas.

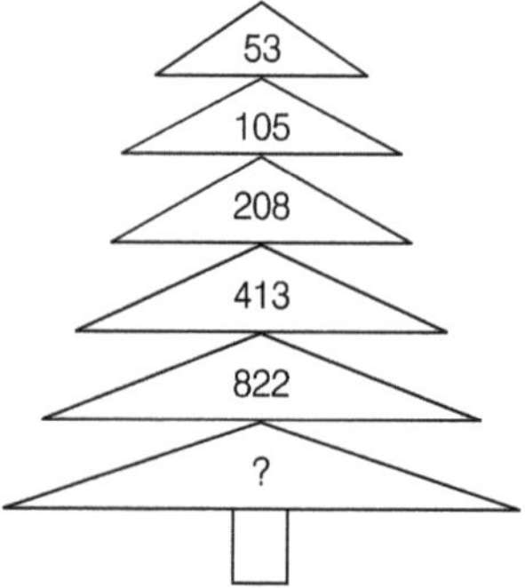

Can you tell me the number of visitors who visited the church this year?

135.

Mary has placed two chocolate cupcakes in one drawer of her kitchen. In another drawer, she has placed a chocolate and a vanilla cupcake; and in a third drawer, two vanilla cupcakes. Her brother knows the arrangement of the cupcakes, but does not know which drawers contain each arrangement.

Mary opens one of the drawers, pulls out a chocolate cupcake and says to her brother, "If you can tell me what the chances are that the other cupcake in this drawer is chocolate, I'll let you have any cupcake you like."

What are the chances that the other cupcake is chocolate?

136.

I asked my son to tell me how many stamps he had. He replied, "The number, if divided by 2 will give a remainder of 1, divided by 3 a remainder of 2, by 4 a remainder of 3, by 5 a remainder of 4, by 6 a remainder of 5, by 7 a remainder of 6, by 8 a remainder of 7, by 9 a remainder of 8, by 10 a remainder of 9."

How many stamps did he have, if he had fewer than 5000 stamps?

137.

Four playing cards are placed in a row. The king of hearts is next to the ace of spades, but not next to the three of diamonds. The three of diamonds is not next to the nine of clubs. Which card is next to the nine of clubs?

138.

Two truck drivers William and Johnson in Los Angeles city have same amount of diesel in their respective trucks. William can drive for 4 hours, whereas Johnson can drive for 5 hours with this amount of diesel.

Both of them start driving from the Los Angeles at the same time. After a few hours, they find out that the amount of diesel remaining in Johnson's the truck is four times the William's truck.

How long did they drive the trucks?

139.

Hero of zero part 2 is the new version of game, where rules have been made little tougher. The participants of this game are required to make any sum equal to zero using the mathematical notation. The four participants were part of the game who used different mathematical notation.

Which participant used the correct mathematical notation, if the expression is $700 - 10 \div \frac{1}{2} \times 35 + 70$ and notation used by 4 participants are as follow?

Participant 1 $\times$ means $\div$, $+$ means $\times$, $\div$ means $+$, $=$ means $-$

Participant 2 $\times$ means $\div$, $+$ means $-$, $\div$ means $\times$, $-$ means $+$

Participant 3 $\times$ means $+$, $+$ means $-$, $\div$ means $\times$, $-$ means $\div$

Participant 4 $\times$ means $\div$, $+$ means $-$, $\div$ means $\times$, $-$ means $+$

140.

I found a very nice handbag in the stop that I thought, I should simply must have. The price was ₹ 10, but I did not have ₹ 10.

The storekeeper was known to me. He said that he had a credit system by which I could pay ₹1 only at the time of purchase and the balance ₹10 could be paid by me at the rate of ₹1 per week for 10 weeks. What annual rate of interest the storekeeper was charging me?

141.

Miss. Banerjee wanted to engage her students in some activity in order to complete some urgent work.

She asked her class to solve a question and the student who will solve it first would be awarded.

Can you tell the correct answer to it?

16	23	28	38	?

142.

To which hexagon below can a dot be added so that both dots then meet the same conditions as in the hexagon above?

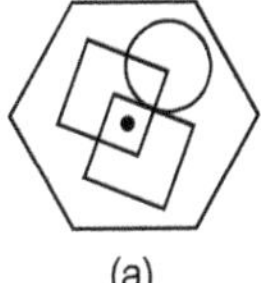
(a)

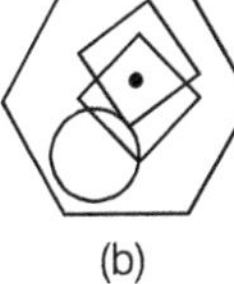
(b)

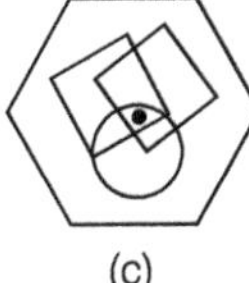
(c)

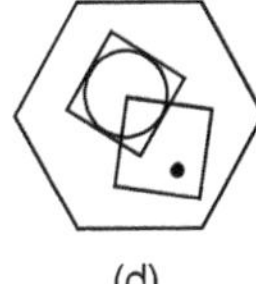
(d)

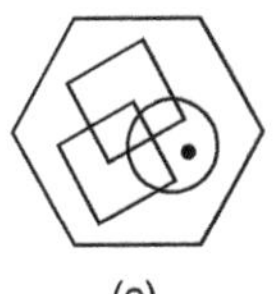
(e)

143.

To reach to a party venue. Mr. Dixit went 60 m North and took a right turn and again moved 16 m ahead.

In order to reach the destination he had to take a right turn and go 48 m ahead instead of this he took a left turn and went 10 m ahead and took a right turn and moved 5 m again taking a right turn and moving 58 m. How far is he from the actual destination?

144.

At feel good Bar and Restaurant, above the kitchen door there are four small lights, arranged side by side and numbered consecutively left to right from one to four. The lights are used to signal waiters when orders are ready. On certain shift there are exactly five waiters—Raman, Pawan, Rakesh, Hitesh and Mithlesh.

- To signal Raman, all four lights are illuminated.
- To signal Pawan, only light one and two are illuminated.
- To signal Rakesh, only light one is illuminated.
- To signal Hitesh, only light two, three and four are illuminated.
- To signal Mithlesh, only light three and four are illuminated.

Can you tell the name of the waiter who is signalled when light two and three are both off?

145.

John's mother told him to go to the river and bring back exactly 9 gallons of water in one trip. She gave him a six gallon bucket and a five gallon bucket to complete his task. Of course, John's mother told him she'd bake his favourite cake if he came back with the 9 gallons.

John had his cake and ate it, too. How was it possible?

146.

Bob likes to prepare personal pizzas. He begins with a circle of dough that is 12 inch in diameter. On top of the dough, he places slices of salami. All of the slices are round and have a 4 inch diameter. If Bob does not overlap the slices or allow any of the slices to extend beyond the edge of the pie, then what is the maximum number of salami slices he can add?

147.

Which is the odd one out?

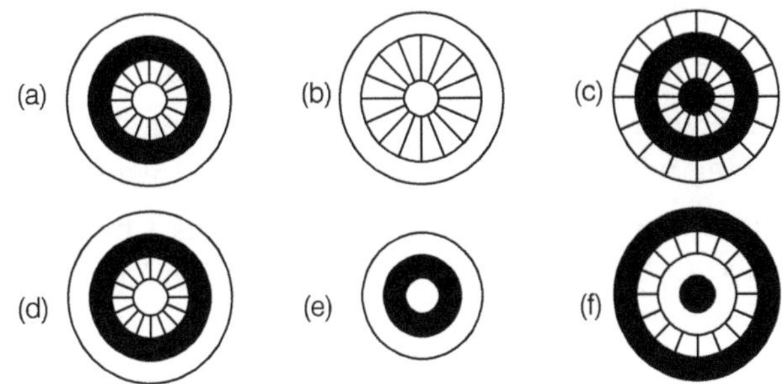

148.

William is playing archery blindfolded. The first arrow he shoots unfortunately misses the bull's eye. The second arrow misses the bull's eye even further. William still shoots a third arrow. How big is the chance that his third shot is also worse than his first shot?

149.

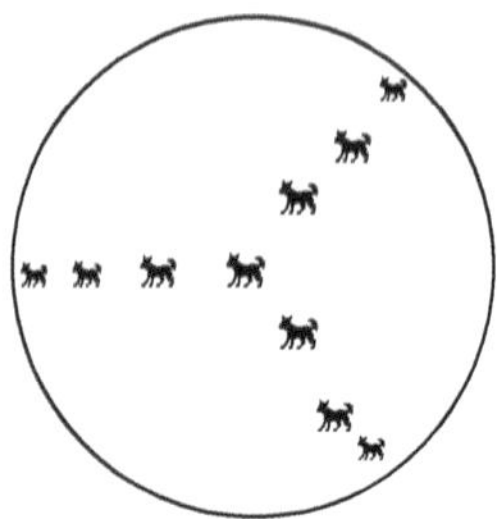

A wizard placed ten cats inside a magic circle as shown in our illustration and hypnotized them, so that they should remain stationary during his pleasure. He then proposed to draw three circles inside the large one, so that no cat could approach another cat without crossing a magic circle. Try to draw the three circles, so that every cat has its own enclosure and cannot reach another cat without crossing a line.

150.

I recently went to a shop and purchased 4 items.

Cost of three of the items: ₹ 1.50, ₹ 3.00, ₹ 4.00

There was a long queue and as I was quite bored, I started playing with my pocket calculator whilst waiting.

Very curiously, the 4 prices of the items I had to purchase added to the same number as I got when I multiplied the 4 prices together.

What was the price of the fourth item?

151.

Herman Rumplemeir, our local butcher, has grown in stature and girth since coming to work here some 30 yr ago. Some interesting facts concerning Herman are:

At age 20 his waist size was 92 cm and his weight was 77 kg.

At age 30 his waist size was 96 cm and his weight was 82 kg.

At age 40 his waist size was 104 cm and his weight was 89 kg.

At age 50 his waist size is 120 cm. What does he weight?

152.

Your boss offers you a choice of two options by which your new salary is to be calculated.

First option Initial salary ₹ 40000 to be increased after each 12 months by ₹ 2000.

Second option Initial salary ₹ 40000 to be increased after each 6 months by ₹ 500.

The salary will be calculated every six months.

Which option should you choose?

153.

Jimmy, the honest newsboy, asked the store owner, if he could buy just the toy and not the egg. The pastry maker told him that the price of the stuffed egg was ₹ 4.50 and that the cost of the egg alone was ₹ 4 more than the cost of the toy inside. How much did Jimmy have to pay for the toy?

154.

Four friends Simon, Lara, Chris and Harry went on a trip, where they need to cross a dark river at night. Unfortunately, they have only one torch and the river is too risky to cross without the torch, if all friends cross simultaneously, then torch light would not be sufficient. Speed of each person of crossing the river is different. Cross time for each person is 1 min, 2 min, 7 min and 10 min. What is the shortest time needed for all four of them to cross the river (if 1 and 2 cross time clasped is 2 min i.e. maximum time can be counted)?

155.

78% of all people are gum chewers and 35% of all people are under the age of 15. If a person has been selected at random, then what is the probability that the person is not a gum chewer and above age 15?

156.

Sara rows down the Snake River at the rate of 4 mph with the current. After she's travelled for two hours, she turns around and rows back against the current to where she started. It takes her four hours to return. What is Sara's rowing rate in still water? What is the rate of Snake River?

157.

In a certain Chinese village live 29 families. Each family has one, two or three bicycles. There are as many families owning three bicycles as families with only one. How many bicycles are there in the village?

158.

Miss. Greg was invited to a friend's anniversary party next week but somehow she lost the invitation card and could not recollect the day of the event. As a result she asked her friend to confirm the day. On not remembering the anniversary day her friend angrily answered, "The day which comes three days after the day which comes two days after the day which comes immediately after the day which comes two days after Monday, is the day my anniversary falls."

What would be the day Miss. Greg should guess to attend the party?

159.

Do you realise that your brain is constantly trying to make sense of the information sent to it by your eyes? You may already know that the image that falls upon the retina of the eye is upside-down. Your brain, however, flips the image over into a more logical upright appearance. Perhaps your brain can flip images 'on cue?'

Which of the choices below is the reflection of the following tile in the mirror?"

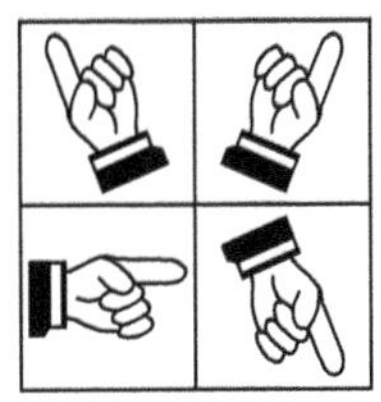

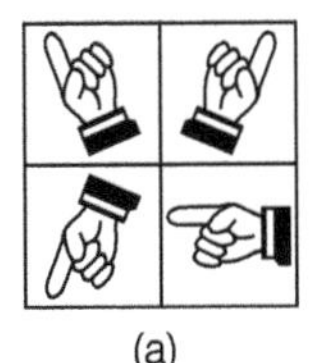

(a)

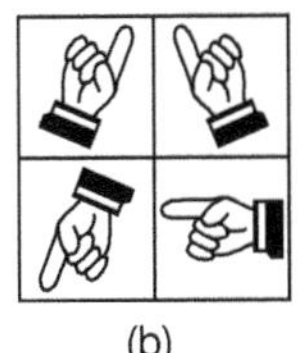

(b)

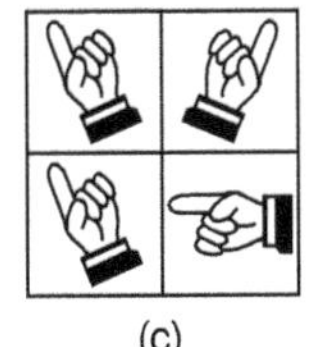

(c)

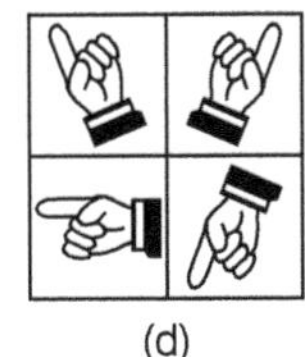

(d)

160.

Mr. Patrick was unwell so a substitute teacher came to teach the class. She asked the students to make correct equations out of the number and signs given in the problem below.

Use each element only once per problem.

Test 2, 3, 6, 8, 8, 16 = ×, ×, /, / ( ) ( )

Example 2, 3, 3, 3, 5, 20 = +, −, ×, ( ), ( )

Answer $5 + (2 \times 3) = 20 - (3 \times 3)$

161.

An engineer goes everyday by train to the city, where he works. At 8:30 am, as soon as he gets off the train, a car picks him up and takes him to the plant. One day the engineer takes a train arriving at 7:00 am, and starts walking towards the plant. On the way, the car picks him up and he arrives at the plant 10 min early.

When does he meet the car?

162.

What number should replace the question mark?

3	8	4	9
2	4	3	6
6	7	8	2
4	2	1	?

163.

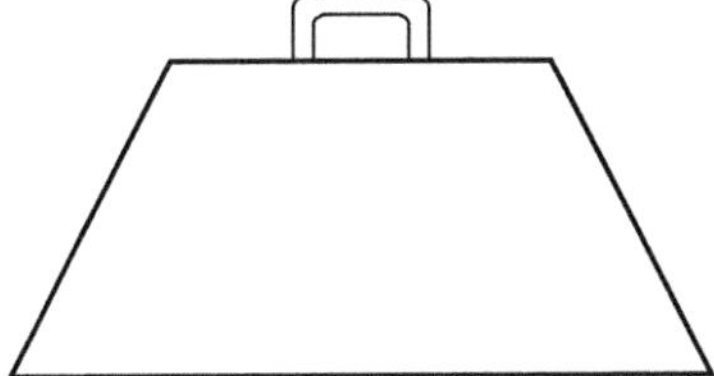

Once upon a time the Hollywood Trunk and Suitcase Company ran a contest with the first prize as an all expenses paid one week trip to Tinseltown. All you had to do, to win the contest, was to divide the outline of a rather unusual suitcase into four parts. All the parts had to be in the same shape and size. However, the shape could not be the same shape as the original suitcase. Let's see if you would be able to make it to the Land of Eternal Youth!

164.

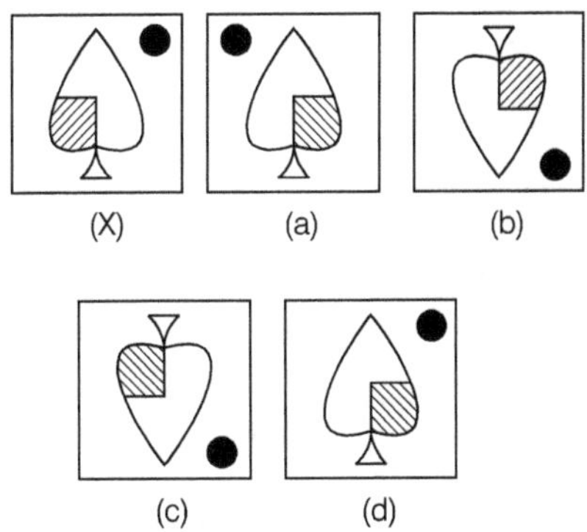

Mr. Robinson is a gambler at Royal Casino in Switzerland. To cheat his opponents he placed a mirror just beside them. When the opponents see their card he was able to see what are the different cards his opponents have.

Which card Mr. Robinson saw actually, if he saw the mirror image of card as shown in the figure (X) of his opponent?

165.

The shape below is formed from three smaller pieces. These pieces are connected by a tiny hinge at their point of attachment. Suppose you were able to rotate the pieces so that neighbouring sides gets aligned flatly and squarely. Which one of the shapes below could this structure look like?

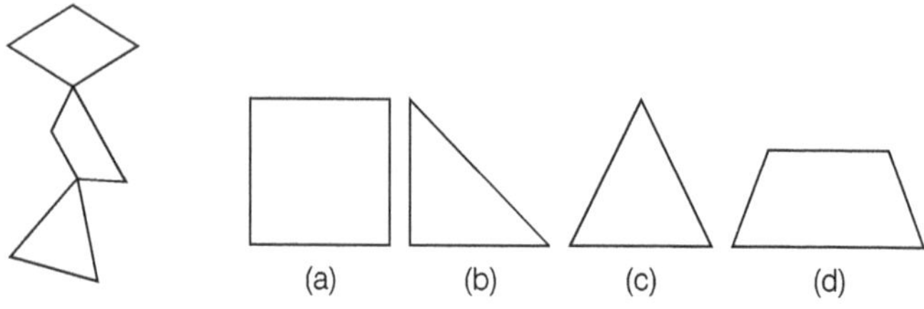

166.

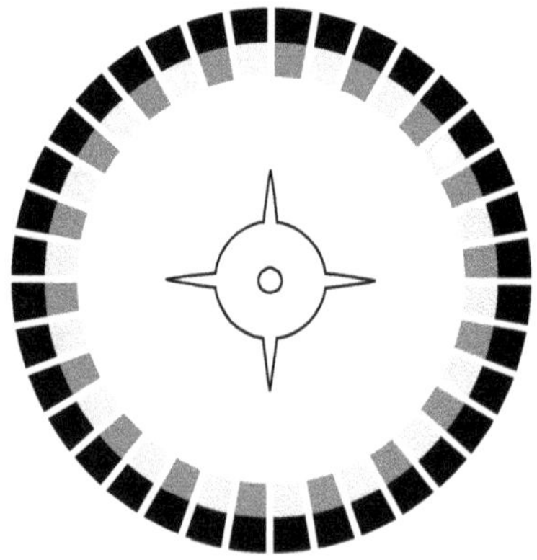

A roulette wheel shows the numbers 1-36. My ball has landed on a particular number that I bet on. It is divisible by 3. When the digits are added together, the total lies between 4 and 8. It is an odd number. When the digits are multiplied together, the total lies between 4 and 8.

Which number have I bet on?

167.

In the game of Hero to Zero, the participants are required to make any sum equal to zero by using the different mathematical notation. There were 4 participants in the game.

Which participant used the correct notation to make the whole sum equal to zero, if the sum is $200 \times 100 + 300 \times 200 - 10 \div 2 + 40$ and the notation used by 4 participants are as follow?

Participant 1 + means '–', – means '×', × means '÷', ÷ means '×'

Participant 2 + means '–', – means '÷', × means '+', ÷ means '×'

Participant 3 + means '×', – means '–', × means '+', ÷ means '×'

Participant 4 + means '÷', – means '+', × means '–', ÷ means '×'

168.

<table>
<tr><td rowspan="2">1</td><td>2</td><td>4</td><td>6</td><td rowspan="2">8</td></tr>
<tr><td>3</td><td>5</td><td>7</td></tr>
</table>

Professor Flunkum has missed his last three classes, because of the new wall-art puzzle that was painted on the building across from his office. The problem seems simple enough, but he can't find the answer. Rearrange numbers one through eight, in the grid, so that no two consecutive digits are adjacent horizontally, vertically or diagonally. It looks as if the professor will have to flunk himself on this one.

169.

Postman Pat delivers the mail in the small village Tenhouses. This village, as you already suspected, has only one street with exactly ten houses, numbered from 1 to 10.

In a certain week, Pat did not deliver any mail at two houses in the village; at the other houses, he delivered mail three times each. Each working day he delivered mail at exactly four houses.

The sums of the house numbers where he delivered mail were :

On Monday : 18

On Tuesday : 12

On Wednesday : 23

On Thursday : 19

On Friday : 32

On Saturday : 25

On Sunday : he never works

Which two houses did not get any mail that week?

170.

The Sunrise Academy conducted a reasoning olympiad for school students. The entrance to sit for the exam had five questions to be solved. One of which is given below.

473982 is to 1419 and 329684 is to 1418, then 751694 is to ?

Only 50% of the students got selected. Can you determine the answer which the selected students gave?

171.

Insert the numbers 1 to 6 into the circles, so that for any particular circle the sum of numbers in the circles connected directly to it equals the value corresponding to the number, as given in the list.

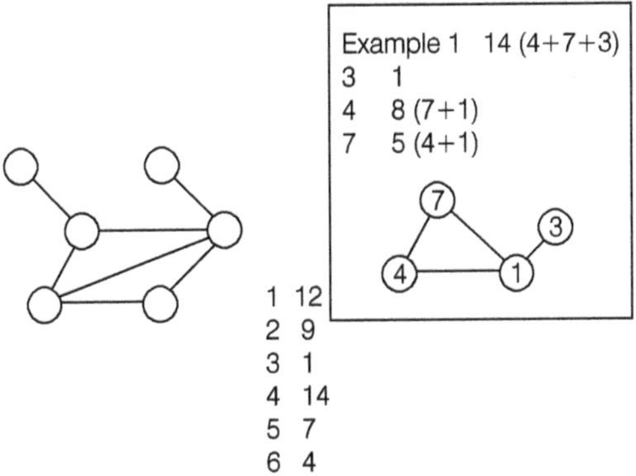

172.

At the zoo the numbers of the animals' cages were

LION	16
SEA LION	27
MONKEY	26
ANTELOPE	32

Find out the number of the buffalo's cage.

173.

In the Parking Area at Cannaught Place 36 vehicles are parked in a parking lot in a single row. After the 1st four-wheeler is one two-wheeler. After 2nd four-wheeler are two, two-wheeler, after the 3rd four-wheeler, there are three two wheelers and so on.

Can you find out the number of two-wheeler in the second half of the row?

174.

The houses on a street are numbered 1, 2, 3, 4, 5, etc., up one side of the street; then the number continue consecutively on the other side of the street and work their way back to be opposite number 1. If house number 12 is opposite house number 29, then how many houses are there on both sides of the street?

175.

Suppose the following pattern was folded up or folded back to form a house. Which one of the structures below can be formed from this pattern?

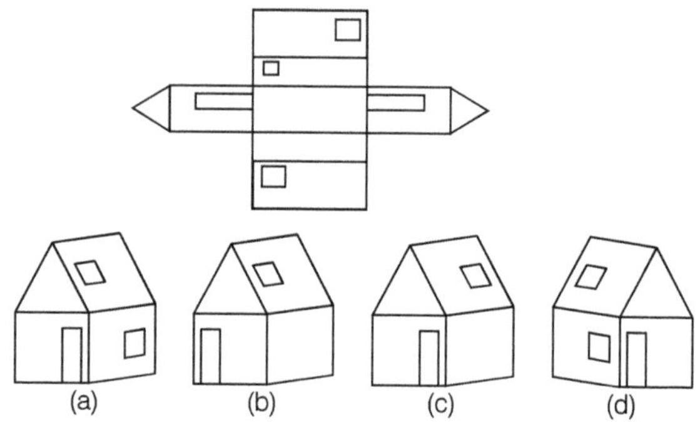

176.

A superstitious pool player did not like number 8 on balls, so he had a number 16 ball specially made instead of number 8 ball. The total number of balls is 15. When he racked the balls up, he always arranged them, so that the number on each ball was the difference of the 2 balls above it. Can you find the arrangement he used?

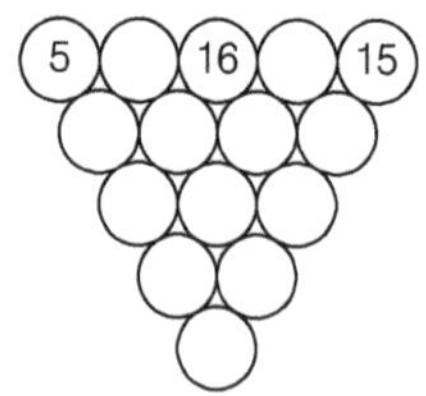

177.

Ramanujam School of mathematics is famous for the talent of its students, who are called Mathematics wizard. They were provided with 4 different problems based on different figures but following the same rule that was closed figures become more and more open and open figures become more and more closed.

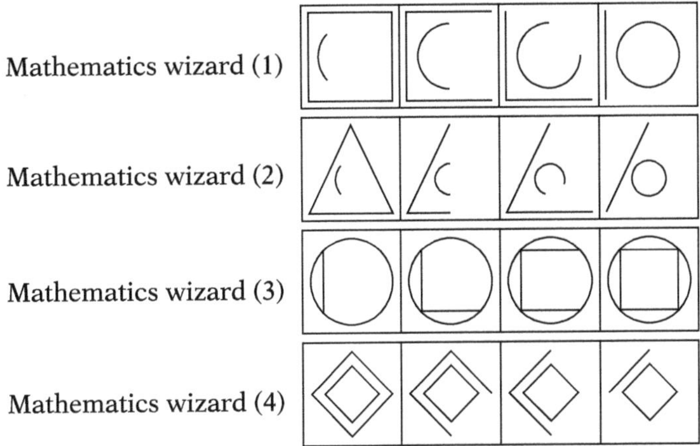

Can you suggest which mathematics wizard solved the problem correctly?

178.

On the eve of valentine day, Archie had to post a love letter to her girlfriend, so he bought a beautiful envelope, which was made by knitting triangle shaped velvet paper.

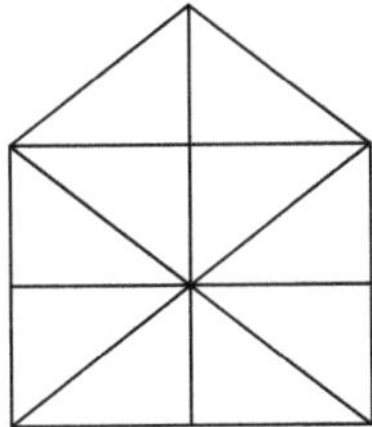

Can you find out how many triangles small or big are inscribed in the envelope?

179.

For a children's book Clarissa creates this crazy 24 h clock with the numbers jumbled and without hands. The numbers are in sequence. Can you crack the number sequence and complete the circle by replacing the question marks with the numbers that fit in the sequence?

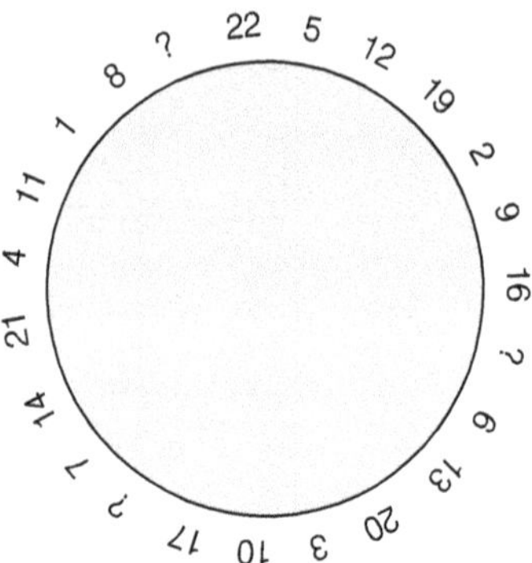

180.

Student philosopher Carlo has found some coasters with the basic mathematical symbols for addition, subtraction, division and multiplication (+, –, ÷, ×) and brings them to the 'Sunset Vue' bar, where he is working for the summer. He arranges the six number coasters as shown below, then asks his manager, Fabrizio, to make a sum by inserting the four symbols (+, –, ÷, ×) between the numbers shown. He tells Fabrizio, "The mathematical symbols can be in any order and only one has been used twice without using the operation rule." Can you help Fabrizio to find the correct answer?

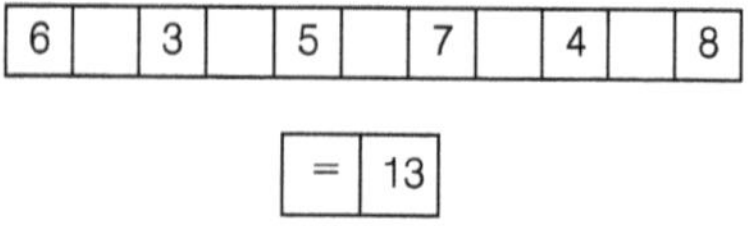

181.

In the given figure, there is a number chain.

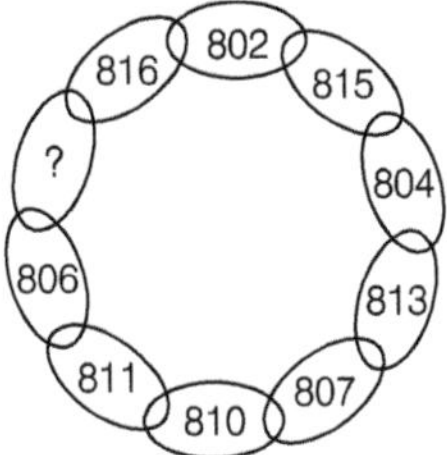

Can you tell me which number would replace the question mark in the number chain?

182.

While reading a certain newspaper, you notice that four pages of one section are missing. One of the missing pages is 13. The back page of this section is 40. What are the other three missing pages?

183.

A man is interrogating his five sons, one of whom has broken a pane of glass in the family greenhouse. Just three of the following statements is proved to be correct. Who broke the glass?

George: Phil broke the glass.

Bill: It was not me.

Al: It was not Ken.

Phil: George is lying.

Ken: Bill is telling the truth.

184.

How many minutes is it before 12 noon, if 55 min ago it was four times as many minutes past 8 am as it is minutes before noon now?

185.

My watch showed the correct time at 12 noon, but then the battery started to run down untill it eventually stopped completely. Between 12 noon up to its stopping, it lost 15 min/h on average. It now shows 6 pm, but it stopped 3 h ago. What is the correct time now?

186.

Ann, Boobie, Cathy and Dave are at their monthly business meeting. Their occupations are author, biologist, chemist and doctor, but not necessarily in that order. Dave just told the biologist that Cathy was on her way with doughnuts. Ann is sitting across from the doctor and next to the chemist. The doctor was thinking that Boobie was a goofy name for parents to choose, but did not say anything.

What is each person's occupation?

187.

Two sisters, Barbara and Monika, celebrate their birthday together, since they were born on the same day and in the same month, except that Barbara is two years younger than Monika. To a tactless question about her age, Monika replied with a smile:

"Barbara is very young– she is not as old as we were together nine years ago. As for me, I am very old, because I am older than we were together nine years ago."

How old is each sister now?

188.

The French Open Tennis Tournament has seven rounds of single elimination of its men's singles competition. This includes the championship match and there are no byes. How many men's singles players originally enter when game begins?

189.

Four burglars were being questioned by the police about a robbery.

"Jack did it," said Alan.

"George did it," said Jack.

"It was not me," said Sid.

"Jack is a liar if he said that I did it," said George.

Only one had spoken the truth. Who was innocent?

190.

Two square floors had to be covered by 12 inch tiles. The number of tiles used was 850. Each side of one floor was 10 ft more than the other floor. What were the dimensions of the two floors?

191.

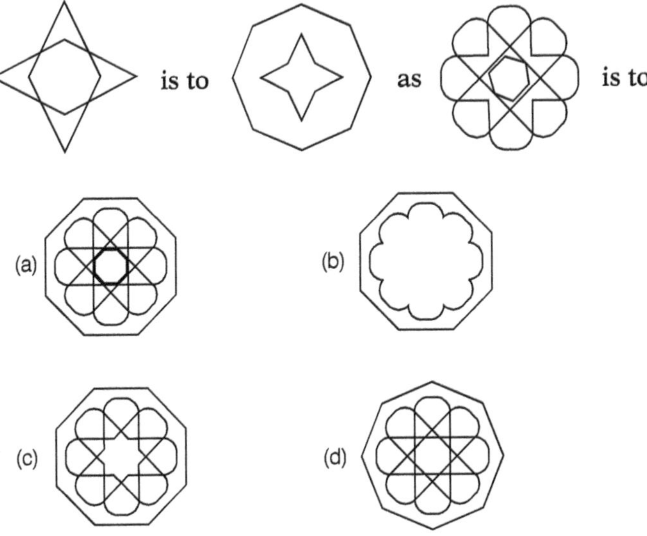

192.

There are all sorts of patterns. Here is one that is based upon a sequence in which some sort of change occurs over time.

Can you uncover how this sequence of tiles changes? If so, use what you have visualised to identify the fourth member of this series.

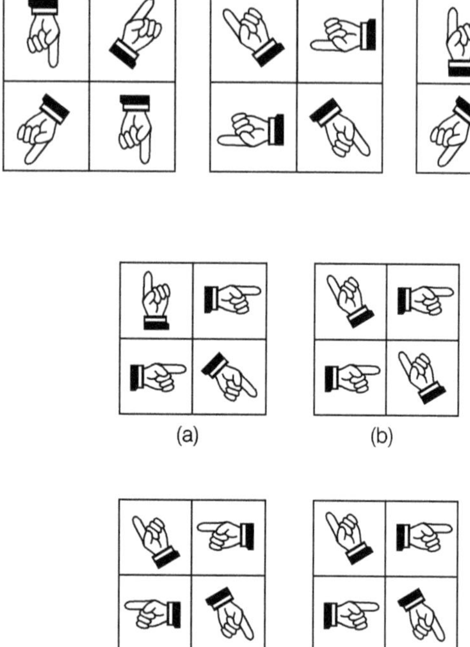

193.

Tom wrote down two positive integers consisting of the digits 1, 2, 3, 4, 5 and 6. Each of the digits appeared in only one of the two numbers and only once. When Tom added up these numbers, he obtained 750. What positive integers did Tom write?

194.

If $A = 2$ and $B + P + F = 24$, what are the values of Q and S?
Hint Consider whole numbers only.

$A + B = Z$

$Z + P = T$

$T + A = F$

$F + S = Q$

$Q - T = 7$

195.

How many ways are there to travel from *A* to *B* following the arrows?

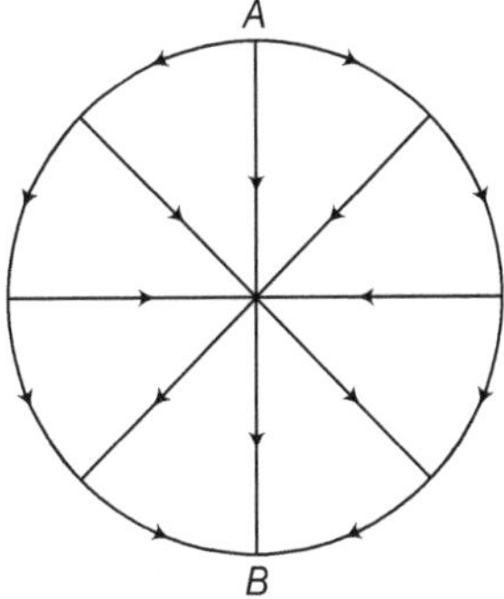

196.

If you add the square of Tony's age to the age of Margaret, the sum is 62. If you add the square of Margaret's age to the age of Tony, the result is 176. What are Tony's and Margaret's ages?

197.

Four cheese pieces of different sizes are placed on stool A. How many moves will it take to move the cheese pieces one by one to stool C? A cheese must not be placed on a cheese smaller than itself.

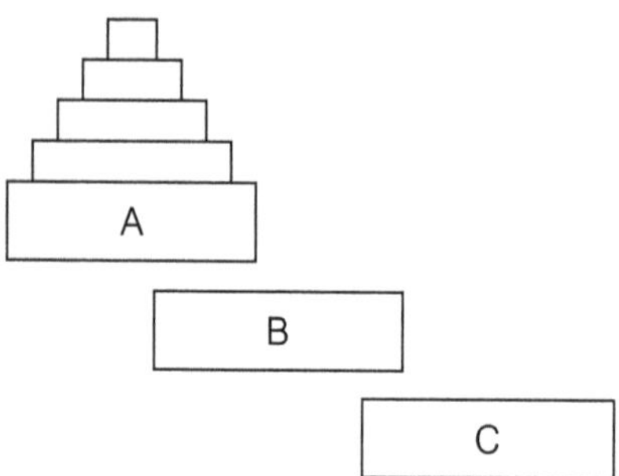

198.

A large square had an area of 490 sq ft. It was the same area as two smaller squares. One had a side that was 3 times the length of the other. What were the areas of the two smaller squares?

199.

What number is two places away
from itself less 3, two places away
from itself plus 2, two places away
from itself plus 4, three places away
from itself less 1, and three places away from itself less 5?

10	24	1	27	9
2	11	5	7	3
29	16	25	12	18
17	14	8	4	13
9	20	22	6	15

200.

Arrange the number 1 to 9 in the boxes below, so that each line of 3 boxes sums to 14. Three numbers have already been placed.

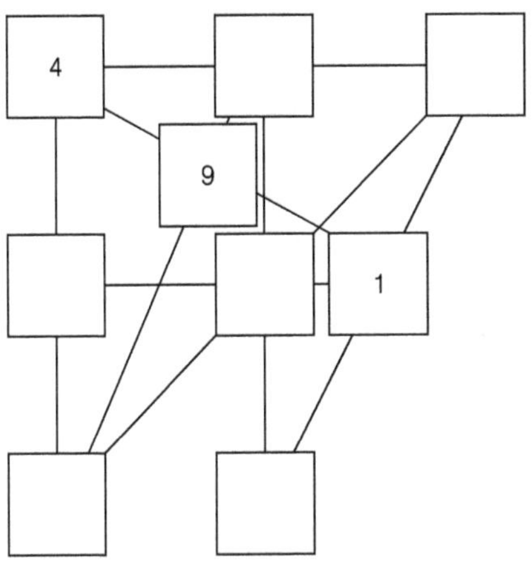

201.

Al, Bob, Cal, Dot and Ed all bought items from the mail-order magazine. Al and Bob paid ₹150, Bob and Cal paid ₹ 200, Cal and Dot paid ₹170, Dot and Ed paid ₹ 210, and Ed and Al paid ₹100. How much did each person spend?

202.

What digits should be substituted for A and B to obtain a correct equation: $AB \times A \times B = BBB$, where AB is a two-digit number and BBB is a three-digit one?

203.

Indian Railway has started exclusive train ticket services for its passengers. When I reached near the ticket counter I found 7 passengers namely A, B, C, D, E, F and G are standing in queue in front of the ticket counter. The number of people standing in front of A is same as the number of people standing behind C. The number of people standing in front of G is same as the number of people standing behind D. Three people are standing between B and F. B is standing behind A, but ahead of E.

Can you tell me, which passenger is standing at the front end of the queue?

204.

India TV organised a great debate for discussion of Budget 2014 and invited representatives from all section of the society. There were twelve persons sitting in two parallel lines in such a way that there are six persons in each row at equidistance. A, B, C, D, E and F are sitting in row 1 and they face towards East. P, Q, R, S, T and V are sitting in row 2 and they face towards West. One person of one row faces the other person of the other row.

P, who is sitting at one of the ends of the row, is second to the right of T. A does not face P or T. A is third to the left of F. There are two persons between Q and V. There is only one person between C and D. C and D do not face P. B is neighbour of C. S, who does not face D, is not the neighbour of Q.

Can you determine how many persons are sitting between E and C?

205.

A. 2^{65}

B. $(2^{64} + 2^{63} + 2^{62} + \quad + 2^{2} + 2^{1} + 2^{0})$

On comparing the values of A and B, which of these statements is correct?

B is 2^{64} larger than A.

A is 2^{64} larger than B.

A and B are equal.

B is larger than A by 1.

A is larger than B by 1.

206.

My friend lives on a long road where the numbers of the houses run consecutively from 1 to 82. To find his number, I asked him three questions to which I received either a 'yes' or 'no' answer to each. The questions were:

1. Is it under 41?
2. Is it divisible by 4?
3. Is it a square number?

My friend answered 'yes' twice and 'no' once. From my friend's answers, I was able to determine for certain what the house number was. What is the house number?

207.

In my wardrobe all but four of my jackets are brown, all but four are blue, all but four are grey, all but four are green and all but four are black. How many jackets do I have altogether?

208.

During Prohibition, Swifty O'Brian was the fastest booze runner on Chicago's North Side. Here we see Swifty delivering twenty cases of Big Benny's finest hooch to four of his select clients. The drops went like this:

Hanratty's received two more cases than the Dutchman's Cafe.

Edna's Hide-a-Way received six less cases than Sal's Saloon.

Sal's Saloon received two more cases than Hanratty's.

The Dutchman's Cafe received two more cases than Edna's Hide-a-Way.

How many cases did each of these watering holes receive?

209.

Recently I visited Khatauli village in Uttar Pradesh, where people have their traditional farming business and have invested their money in a finance company, which has promised them a good return in the 6th month and people were expecting good return.

Can you tell them what amount will they receive in 6th month, if their money is growing in the following manner?

1st month	₹ 10000
2nd month	₹ 11000
3rd month	₹ 9900
4th month	₹ 10890
5th month	₹ 9801
6th month	?

210.

During my first marriage anniversary, my wife Anushka prepared six exquisite dishes A to F, among which two are starters, two are main course and two are desserts and were arranged in circular order. A is adjacent to F, C is not adjacent to either B or E. D is the main course and is adjacent to desserts. Both the starters are adjacent to each other. A is opposite to desserts, which is not B.

Can you tell me my wife has placed which dish opposite to E?

211.

Use numerical logic to crack the number sequence and complete the number board grid by replacing the question marks with the numbers that fit in the sequence.

10	11	9	10	8
?	5	6	4	9
11	?	6	8	7
13	12	?	13	15

212.

Exactly how many minutes is it before 7 O'clock, if 40 min ago it was three times as many minutes past 2 O'clock?

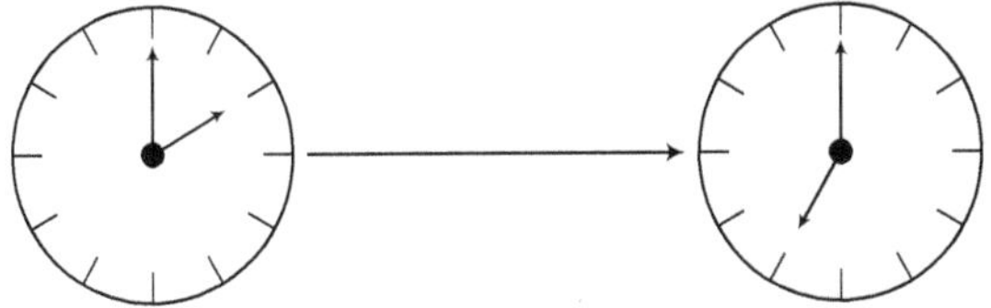

213.

I am thinking of a number between 99 and 999.

1. The number is below 500.
2. It is a square number.
3. It is a cube number.
4. The first and last digits are 5, 7 or 9.

One of the first three statements is a lie. What is the number?

214.

Calvin Collectible hit the jackpot the other day when he came across a trove of old steel mechanical toys. Included were dump trucks, steam shovels and farm tractors. Let's make a puzzle of his find. He bought the following four lots of toys:

The first lot had 1 tractor, 3 shovels and 7 trucks and sold for ₹ 140.

The second lot had 1 tractor, 4 shovels and 10 trucks and sold for ₹ 170.

The third lot had 1 tractor, 1 shovel and 5 trucks and sold for ₹ 100.

The fourth lot had 10 tractors, 15 shovels and 25 trucks.

The fifth lot had 1 tractor, 1 shovel and 1 truck.

The problem is to figure out how much Calvin paid for lots number four and fifth.

215.

This puzzle requires analytical reasoning. Determine the relationships between the figures and words to find two solutions.

○○○ = LAG

◇◇ = LEB

◇◇◇ = ?

RAB = ○ ○ (stacked vertically)

REG = ◇ ◇ ◇ (stacked vertically)

REBRAG = ?

216.

At the cake shop, there are three types of cakes with their prices in round rupees. For a rupee, you can get a cream cake, two fruit cakes or three doughnuts. Two brothers, Jeremy and Roger, had been given ₹ 11 by their parents and invited a group of backyard kids to have cakes together. The group consisted of as many boys as girls. Each kid was treated to the same set of cakes, which consisted of the same number of the same cakes. How big was the group of kids?

217.

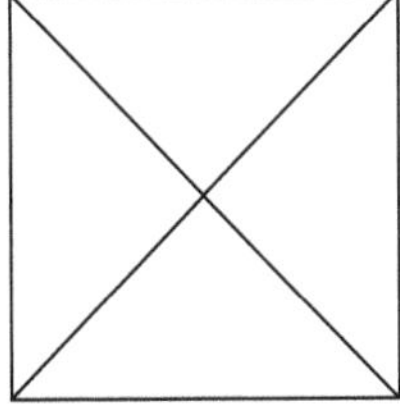

To solve this puzzle, come up with an unconventional solution to what, at first glance, will seem to be an impossible problem. Take all the numbers 1 through 9 and place them in two diagonals, so that the sum of each diagonals will be the same.

218.

Snow white and the seven dwarfs, fed up with being pestered by autograph hunters, changed their names and went off to work– all eight of them, one behind the other– confident that now they would not be recognised. There were two places between Florence and Ernie, while Gertie was immediately in front of Henry. Celia was three places in front of Daniel and there were two places between Andrea and Brian. Brian was somewhere in front of Florence, Henry was somewhere in front of Celia and Ernie was immediately in front of Andrea. Perhaps they should have changed their clothes as well because a fan ran up to the fourth from the front and shouted "You're Dopey!"

What was Dopey's pseudonym?

219.

Can you uncover the pattern in this 'tree' and use it solve for the missing number.

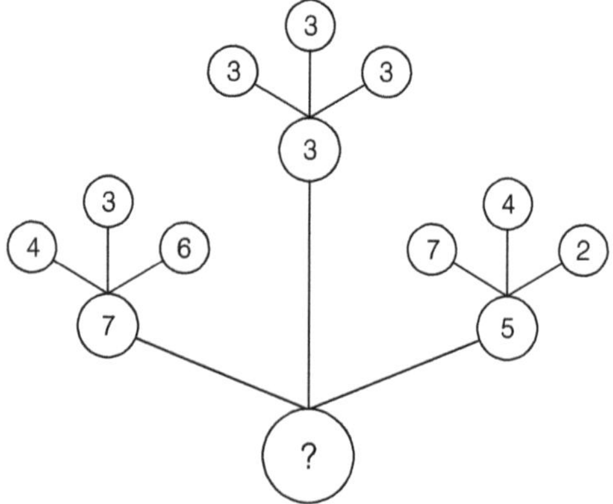

220.

Someone had made a mistake decorating the coaster. Can you find the wrong pattern?

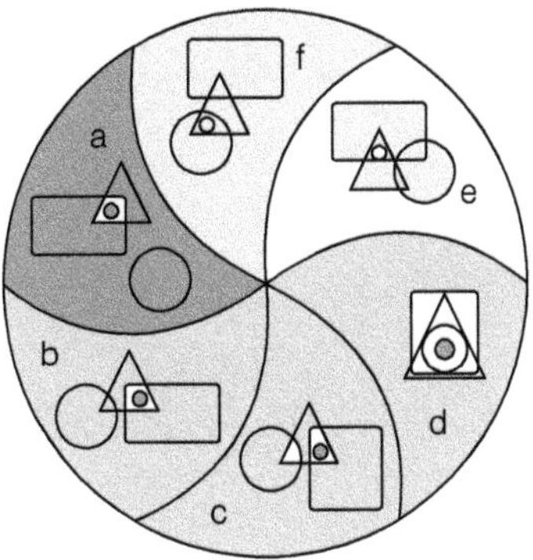

221.

To which of these diagrams could you add a circle to match the conditions of the figure at the top?

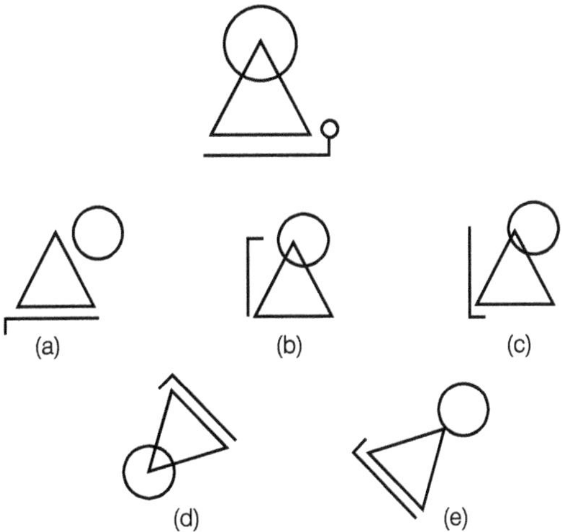

222.

Surveen, Jasmin and Japneet join a running race. The distance is 2000 m. Surveen beats Jasmin by 30 m and Japneet by 100 m. By how much could Jasmin beat Japneet over the full distance, if they both ran as before?

223.

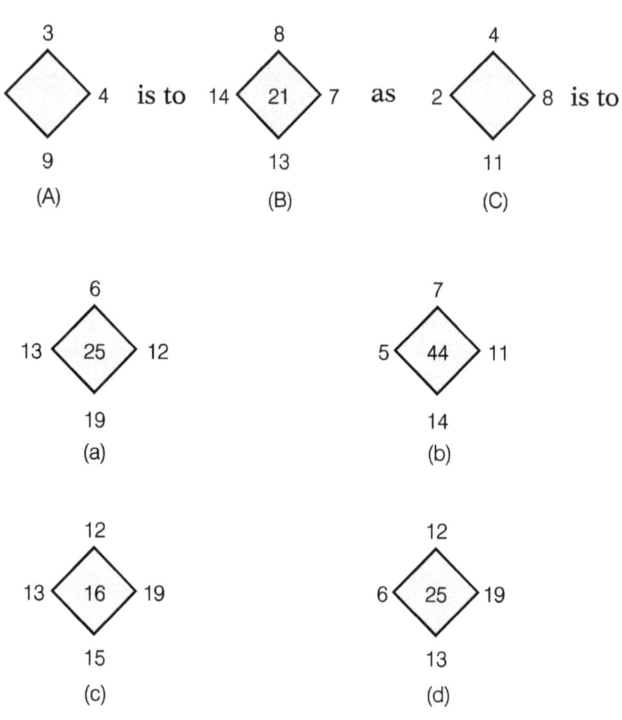

224.

Mr. Brick in his Mathematics class asked student to solve a different type of puzzle. He gave them digits from 1 to 9, 7 plus and minus sign and showed them how to obtain hundred '100' from it as given below.

$$1 + 2 + 3 - 4 + 5 + 6 + 7 + 8 + 9 = 100$$

He then asked the class to think of an arrangement using the same digits and with only three plus and minus signs?

225.

Catherine sold watermelons in the market. 'The first customer, Ms. Angela, bought half the watermelons there were and a half of one. The second customer, Ms. Barbara, bought half of the remaining fruit and the very half Ms. Angela had left behind. The third customer, Ms. Cindy, again bought half of what remained and a half of one fruit.

As there were no takers for the last watermelon, Catherine brought it home. What were her day's takings, if she sold the fruit at 2 dollars a piece?

Explanations

1. Here, the numbers from 0 to 9 are coded by 'PSICHOLAZY', so each number has a specific code given as follows:

Numbers	0	1	2	3	4	5	6	7	8	9
Codes	P	S	I	C	H	O	L	A	Z	Y

Now, to find the code for ₹ 875.50, we have

$$8 \longrightarrow Z$$
$$7 \longrightarrow A$$
$$5 \longrightarrow O$$
$$0 \longrightarrow P$$
$$875.50 \longrightarrow ZAO.OP$$

Hence, the code for the commodity having cost equal to ₹ 875.50 is ZAO.OP.

2. The letters which are symmetrical and will look the same in the mirror are as follows

A H I M O T U V W X Y

According to above, only boy 4 has given the correct collection of letters whose mirror image will be same.

i.e. Boy 4 : A O V I V O A

3. Let the number of men be x.

According to the question,

Number of women $= 3x$

and number of children $= 2x$

Also, total number of people $= 30$

According to the question,

$$x + 3x + 2x = 30$$
$$\Rightarrow \quad 6x = 30$$
$$\Rightarrow \quad x = 5$$

Hence, there are 5 men, 10 children and 15 women available in the party.

4. Given, four girls are sitting on a bench to be photographed, facing towards North as follows

I. Shikha is to the left of Reena.

↑ ↑
Shikha Reena

II. Manju is to the right of Reena.

↑ ↑ ↑
Shikha Reena Manju

III. Rita is between Reena and Manju.

↑ ↑ ↑ ↑
Shikha Reena Rita Manju

Now, in photograph the position of the girls will change to their opposite as follows:

Manju, Rita, Reena, Shikha

According to above, Rita is sitting second from the left in the photograph.

Hence, option (d) is correct.

5. In the given figure, D adds up to 36 as shown below:

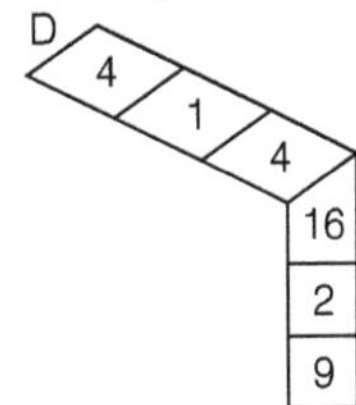

Row A : $7+8+2+9+4+3=33$

Row B : $3+7+8+2+4+9=33$

Row C : $2+4+7+6+3+=33$

Similarly, E, F, G, H, I all add to 33.

While row D : $4+1+4+16+2+9=36$

But all other rows add up to 33.

So, row D is odd one.

6. Let the weight of fish be x kg.

Also, given that the fish weighs $\frac{5}{7}$ kg + $\frac{5}{7}$ of its own weight.

i.e. $\frac{5}{7} \quad + \frac{5}{7}x$

According to the statement,

$$x=\frac{5}{7}+\frac{5}{7}x$$

$$\Rightarrow \quad x-\frac{5}{7}x=\frac{5}{7} \quad \Rightarrow \quad \frac{7x-5x}{7}=\frac{5}{7}$$

$$\Rightarrow \quad \frac{2}{7}x=\frac{5}{7} \quad \Rightarrow \quad x=\frac{5}{2}=2\frac{1}{2}\text{ kg}$$

So, the fish weighs $2\frac{1}{2}$ kg.

7. By using hit and trial method, consider

$$5 \times 2 - 3 + 5 \div 4 = 3$$

Now, using the operation from left to right, we get

$$5 \times 2 = 10$$

$$10 - 3 = 7$$

$$7 + 5 = 12$$

and $\quad 12 \div 4 = 3$

which equals to right hand side.

8. Given integers 1 to 9 are assigned to

L, M, N, O, P, Q, R, S, T and P = 4

Also, given $T - P = 5$

$\Rightarrow \quad T - 4 = 5$

$\Rightarrow \quad T = 9$

and $\quad T - N = 3$

$\Rightarrow \quad 9 - N = 3$

$\Rightarrow \quad N = 6$

So, the value of N or the number assigned to N is 6.

9. In the given figure, add the numbers from top to bottom diagonally to the left of the bottom line for the first three positions on the bottom line and to the right for the next three positions as shown below:

From left, $\quad 4 + 7 + 8 + 5 + a = 28$

$\Rightarrow \quad a + 24 = 28 \quad \Rightarrow \quad a = 4$

From right, $\quad 4 + 3 + d + 6 + 5 = 20$

$\Rightarrow \quad d + 18 = 20 \quad \Rightarrow \quad d = 2$

Similarly, $\quad 7 + 6 + c + 6 = 24$

$c + 19 = 24 \quad \Rightarrow \quad c = 5$

and $\quad 8 + 4 + 8 = b \quad \Rightarrow \quad b = 20$

10. The identification mark (X) is inscribed in the ball number 4, so the ball which belonged to the boy is number 4.

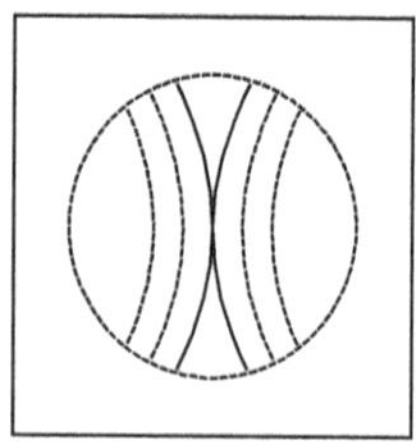

11. Since, Imran saw the number through the side window mirror, so he would have noted down the mirror image of the actual number. In order to find out the actual number, the mirror image of the noted down number is to be found.

BR1LS9765

So, the correct number of the car is **B R 1 L S 9 7 6 5**.

12. For the white shapes to be adjacent triangle and circle should be together.

Since, the star has moved one place, so it can be either move to one left side or right side.

Now, for square to be between the circle and the star, the star should be at the end, therefore the required sequence is

13. Time taken by hot tap to fill the bathtub = 4.5 min

Time taken by cold tap to fill the bathtub =12 min

Time taken by plug hole to empty the bathtub =18 min

We need to find the work done by each in 1 min

i.e. work done (filling the bathtub) by hot tap in 1 min = $\frac{1}{4.5}$

Work done (filling the bathtub) by cold tap in 1 min = $\frac{1}{12}$

and work done (empty the bathtub) by plug hole = $\frac{1}{18}$

Now, the part filled in 1 min

$$= \frac{1}{4.5} + \frac{1}{12} - \frac{1}{18}$$

$$= \frac{10}{45} + \frac{1}{12} - \frac{1}{18}$$

$$= \frac{40 + 15 - 10}{180} = \frac{45}{180} = \frac{1}{4}$$

$\therefore$ Total time taken to fill the bathtub = 4 min

14. According to the given information,

I. pa < ni

II. re > sa

III. re > ma > sa

IV. ga > re > ma > sa > ni > pa

So, 'pa' is the lowest note sung by Tansen.

15. As per the information, the direction map is as follows:

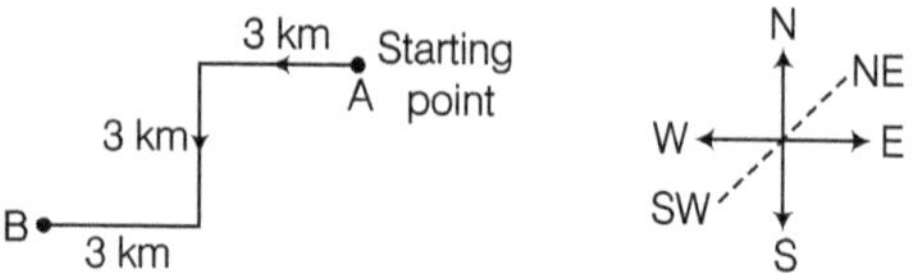

As per the direction map, point B (end point) is towards the South-West direction from point A (starting point).

So, Sachin is walking towards South-West direction.

Hence, option (b) is correct.

16. The main figure gets upside down in the next figure having circle at the bottom inside it with opposite colour black/white of the circle and figure both.

In the third figure, the white circle is outside and the figure is in black colour, so the fourth figure will be upside down form of the third figure having a black circle inside it at the bottom with colour of the figure being white

i.e. 

Hence, option (c) is correct.

17. The required letter will be chosen through the following steps:

I. The letter which is third to the right of C is F.

II. The letter which is immediate left to F is E.

III. The letter which is second to the right of E is G.

So, the first letter of the person's name is 'G'.

18. In the given set of words, the first letter of the next word is one letter ahead of the last letter of the previous word, such as follows and the length of word increases by one each time:

Hence, the word 'TRUCULENT' comes next.

19. In all the figures, the line has turned four times whereas in figure (c), the line has turned five times, so the figure (c) is odd one.

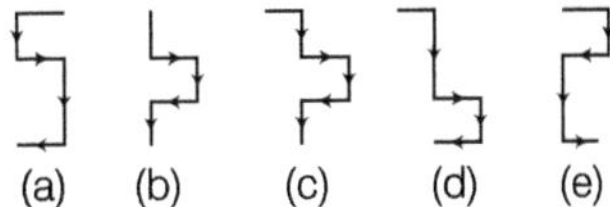

20. The words are as follow:

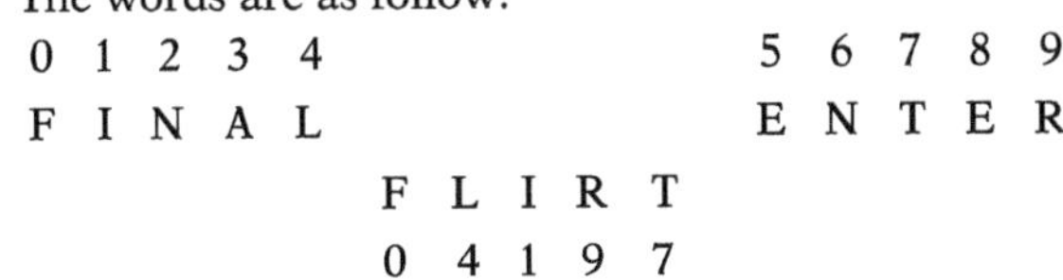

0	1	2	3	4	5	6	7	8	9
F	I	N	A	L	E	N	T	E	R

F L I R T

0 4 1 9 7

On the basis of the above, we have

B	I	K	E	R	R	I	F	L	E
0	1	2	3	4	5	6	7	8	9

0 4 1 9 7

B R I E F

So, the required word is BRIEF.

Hence, option (c) is correct.

21. The water image of the number of ship is given as follows:

∩Ƨə⅂Ơ߈WƧM3

The correct number of ship will be obtained on looking at the water image of the above number as follows:

∩Ƨə⅂Ơ߈WƧM3

US91Q4M5W3

22. We unfold the paper in this manner and get the required result.

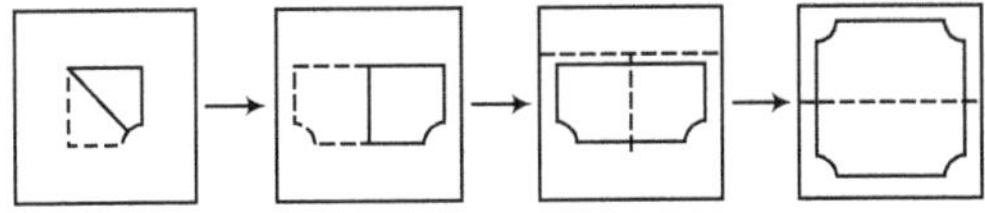

Hence, option (d) is correct.

23. Given that, the perimeter of one square $= 100$ inch

So, the side of the square $= 25$ inch

Total number of edges $= 25$

Number of common edges $= 7$

$\therefore$ Outside edges which make its shape $= 25 - 7 = 18$

$\therefore$ Perimeter of the shape $= 25 \times 18 = 450$ inch

24. There are the prime numbers from 17 to 41. So, question mark (?) replaced by 41.

25. The water image seen by IAEA spy of the word NUCLEAR is as follows:

N U C L E A R

И ∩ C Γ E ∀ ʁ

26. In the first stage, the figure which is repeated twice is the outer shape in the second stage.

The figure which came once in first stage is repeated twice in second.

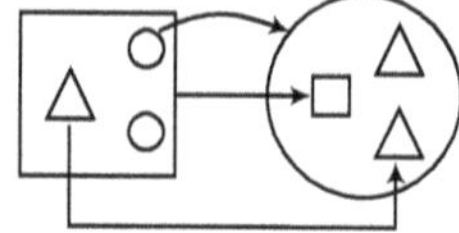

In the second to third stage, the same rule is as follows:

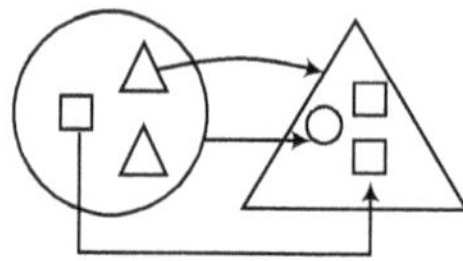

So, the fourth figure will be

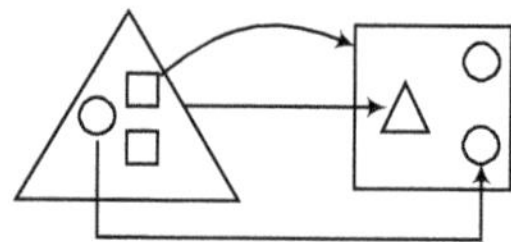

So, option (b) is correct.

27. The mirror image of the car number is

DL9CG4728 | 8274GC9LD (mirrored)

Figure (c) matches the correct image of the number.

Hence, option (c) is correct.

28. The number of the plane can be obtained by finding the water image of the number noted.

Λ∀⅄∩ 8 4 3 6 (inverted)

VAYU 8436

29. The number of apples and bags can be find out by finding the factors of 667 which are as follow:

$$667 = 29 \times 23$$

So, 667 is the product of two prime numbers in which 23 is smaller.

So, the number of bags $= 23$ and number of apples in each bag $= 29$

30. The day when each one will return at the same time can be found by calculating the least common multiple of the days they travel home.

$$(5,7,6) = 210$$

So, each one of them will return back on 210th day at the same time.

31. According to the information,

Hillary > Al > Bill

Hillary > Chelsea > Bill

As per the above information, Bill always loses against any of the player, so Bill is the weakest player.

32. They are letters K, L, M and N on their side. So,○ is the next one.

Hence, option (b) is correct.

33. The different names given to animals are

Animals who can walk → swimmers

Animals who crawl → flying

Animals who lives in water → snakes

Animals who fly in the sky → hunters

Now, lizard crawls, so it will be called a 'flying' animal.

34. The maximum possible chance when different apples will come out is three.

A type	B type	C type	I/II/III type
I turn	II turn	III turn	IV turn

So, atleast 2 apples of one kind will be taken out on maximum 4 chances.

Now, to have three apples of one kind, following possibility will be considered.

A	B	C	A	B	C	A/B/C
I turn	II turn	III turn	IV turn	V turn	VI turn	VII turn

So, 3 apples of one kind will be taken out on maximum 7 chances.

35. Given,

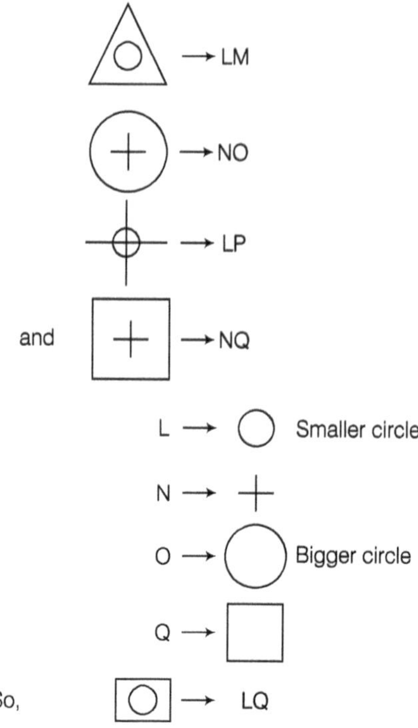

36. The mobile has the following pattern of IMEI number

First letter, $J \xrightarrow{1} K \xrightarrow{1} L \xrightarrow{1} \textcircled{M} \xrightarrow{1} N \xrightarrow{1} O$

Middle number, $2 \xrightarrow{2} 4 \xrightarrow{3} 7 \xrightarrow{4} \textcircled{11} \xrightarrow{5} 16 \xrightarrow{6} 22$

Third letter, $Z \xrightarrow{-2} X \xrightarrow{-2} V \xrightarrow{-2} \textcircled{T} \xrightarrow{-2} R \xrightarrow{-2} P$

So, 4th IMEI number will be 'M11T'.

37. The letters which Aslesha spoke are

adb_/ac_d/a_cd/dcb_/dbc_/cbda

Fill in the missing letter out of a, b, c, d and the pattern will be as follows:

adb$\underline{c}$/ac$\underline{b}$d/a$\underline{b}$cd/dcb$\underline{a}$/dbc$\underline{a}$/cbda

So, the missing letters are cbbaa.

38. According to the given steps in the figures as shown below:

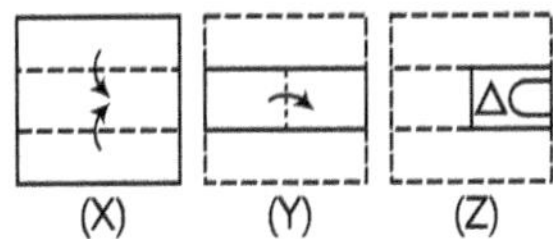

The correct unfolded form of figure (Z) has given by student 2, i.e.

student (2) .

39. Here, the rule which is being followed is reversed the second number (the number after the plus sign) and then add the resultant which gives the required answer.

$$14 + 55 \rightarrow 14 + 55 \rightarrow 69$$
$$28 + 23 \rightarrow 28 + 32 \rightarrow 60$$
$$22 + 31 \rightarrow 22 + 13 \rightarrow 35$$
$$17 + 28 \rightarrow 17 + 82 \rightarrow 99$$
$$41 + 27 \rightarrow 41 + 72 \rightarrow 113$$

So, the question mark (?) will be replaced by 113.

40. By the given relation,

(1) & ⟶ + (3)
(2) * ⟶ # (4)
(3) + ⟶ & (1)
(4) # ⟶ * (2)

So, + > # = is to

(1) + ⟶ (3) #
(2) > ⟶ (4) =
(3) # ⟶ (1) +
(4) = ⟶ (2) >

Hence, obtion (b) is correct.

41. If a third diagonal, BC is drawn, this completes an equilateral triangle. All its sides are equal, because they are cube diagonals. Being equilateral, all its angles are 60°.

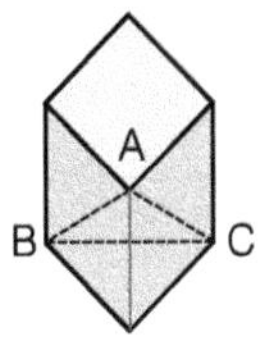

42. By removing the middle stick from each of the outer edge of the given arrangements, we will get an arrangement with five squares.

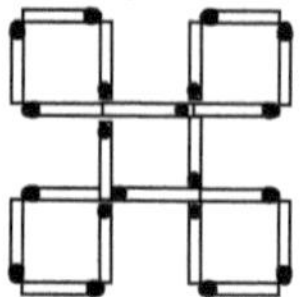

43. The figure rotates 90° clockwise at each stage and a different section is shaded in turn.

Hence, option (d) is correct.

44. The digit in the middle of third figure is equal to the sum of digit in the upper and lower section of first figure,

i.e.

$3842 + 5639 = 9481$

Similarly, $7684 + 1979 = 9663$

$$\therefore \quad 5217 + 4381 = 9598 = \begin{matrix} 9 \\ 5 \\ 9 \\ 8 \end{matrix}$$

45. The pattern is as follows

$$\begin{aligned} B+E+R+L+I+N &= (-100)+300+(-100)+(-100)+300+(-100) \\ &= 200 \text{ miles} \end{aligned}$$

Each vowel is worth 300 and each consonant is worth (−100). These are totalled in each city name to give the distance.

Same pattern will be followed in others:

$$\begin{aligned} C+A+R+D+I+F+F &= (-100)+300+(-100)+(-100) \\ &\quad +300+(-100)+(-100) \\ &= 600-500 = 100 \text{ miles} \end{aligned}$$

So, the distance of CARDIFF will be 100 miles.

46. Anil is the brother of Romi and Romi is the son of Chandra. So, Anil is the son of Chandra. Now, Bimal is the father of Chandra. So, Anil is the grandson of Bimal. Hence, option (b) is correct.

The pictorial representation is

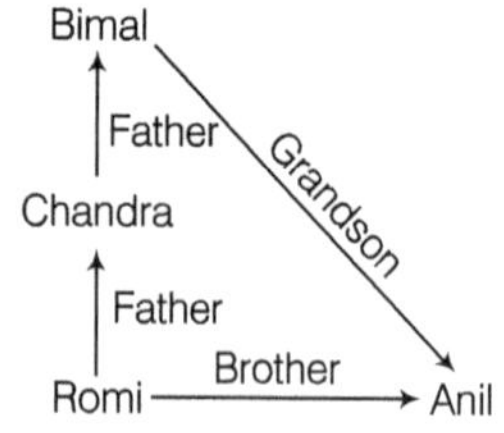

47. Here, the relation between the number are as follows:

I. 2836 : 13

$13 = 2 + 8 - 3 + 6$

II. 9423 : 14

$14 = 9 + 4 - 2 + 3$

III. $? = 7 + 2 - 2 + 9 = 7 + 9 = 16$

So, question mark (?) will be replaced by 16.

48. The ants can only avoid a collision, if they all decide to move in the same direction (either clockwise or anti-clockwise) as shown in the given figure:

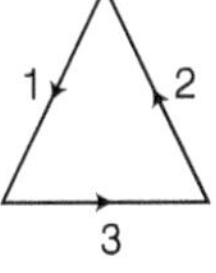

If the ants do not pick the same direction, there will definitely be a collision. Each ant has the option to either move clockwise or anti-clockwise. There is a one in two chance that an ant decides to pick a particular direction. Using simple probability calculations, we can determine the probability of no collision.

P (no collision) = P (all ants go in a clockwise direction)
+ P (all ants go in an anticlockwise direction)

$= 0.5 \times 0.5 \times 0.5 + 0.5 \times 0.5 \times 0.5$

$= 0.125 + 0.125 = 0.25$

49. The correct figure in which three toothpicks will be removed to have four equal squares.

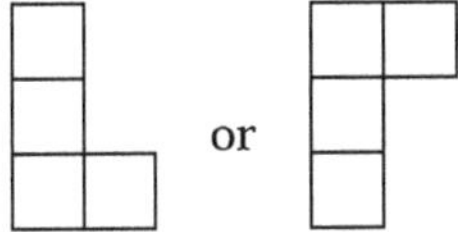

50. Let the cost of one book be ₹ x.

Then, total cost $= 7x$

and money carried by Agatha $= 7x + 5$ ...(i)

Now, the cost of one book is ₹ x.

So, total cost of eight books $= 8x$

$\therefore$ Money carried by Agatha $= 8x - 7$ ...(ii)

From Eqs. (i) and (ii), we get

$$7x + 5 = 8x - 7 \Rightarrow 12 = x$$

$\therefore$ Cost of each book = ₹ 12

and money carried by Agatha $= 7x + 5 = 7 \times 12 + 5$

$= 84 + 5 =$ ₹ 89

51. If the beggar can make a whole cigarette from 6 butts, then he can make 12 cigarettes from the 72 he finds.

Once he smokes those, he then will have another 12 butts, which gives him enough to make another 2 cigarettes.

$\therefore$ Total number of cigarettes $= 12 + 2 = 14$

52. The direction diagram of Mr. Booshi is as follows:

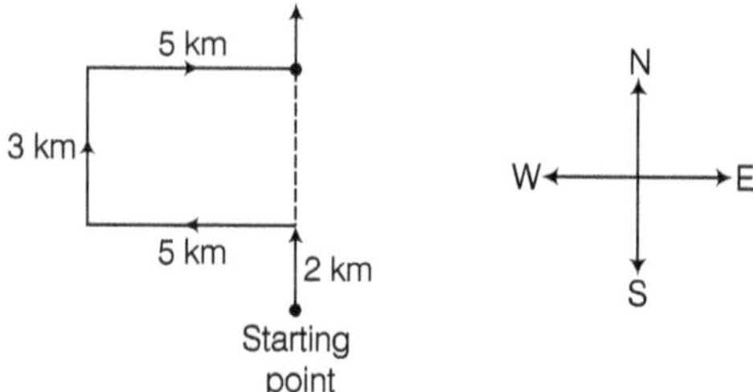

So, the venue was towards the North direction of the point, where Mr. Booshi met the passerby.

53. Pictorial representation of the relation is

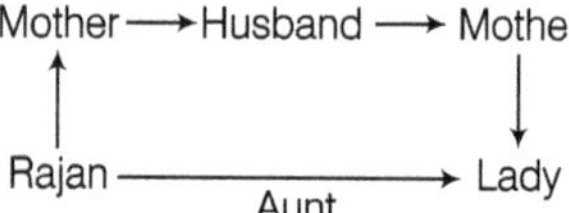

In other words, Rajan's mother's husband is Rajan's father and Rajan's father's
Mother is Rajan's grandmother.
Now, the daughter of Rajan's grandmother will be Rajan's aunt.

54. Difference of the finish and start times of cycle $A = 3:15 - 2:06$

$= 1:09 =$ Start time of cycle B

Difference of the finish and start times of cycle $B = 3:20 - 1:09$

$= 2:11 =$ Start time of cycle C

$\therefore$ Difference of finish and start times of cycle $C = 5:24 - 2:11$

$= 3:13 =$ Start time of cycle D

So, question mark (?) will be replaced by 3 : 13.

55. The number of the horse is equal to the difference of the weight handicap.

i.e. No. $4 = (5 - 1) = 4$

No. $3 = (4 - 1) = 3$

No. ? $= (4 - 2) = 2$

Hence, the missing number is No. 2.

56. Each of the number in the outermost string is equal to the difference between the numbers in outer and inner circles moving clockwise.

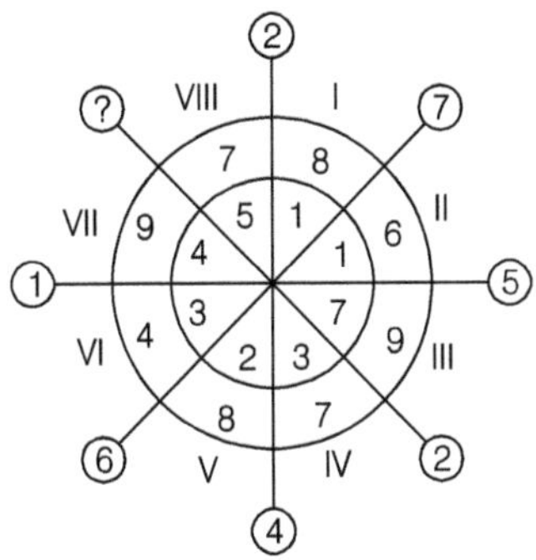

I $= 8 - 1 = 7$ II $= 6 - 1 = 5$

III $= 9 - 7 = 2$ IV $= 7 - 3 = 4$

V $= 8 - 2 = 6$ VI $= 4 - 3 = 1$

? = VII $= 9 - 4 = 5$

So, the missing number is 5.

57. Here, codes are given to different commands which have the following meaning:

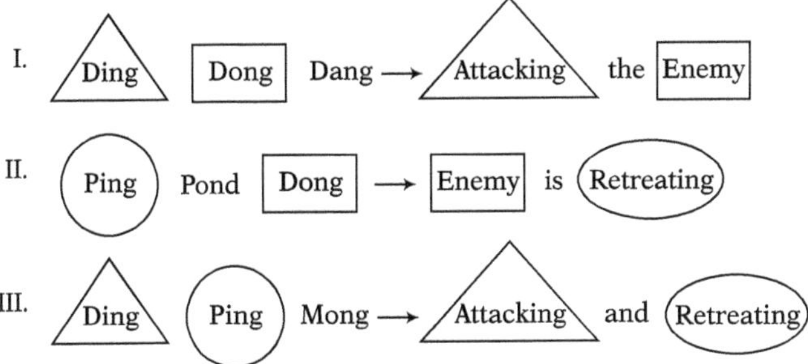

So, from I and II, we have 'Dong' stands for 'enemy'.

58. The sequence is formed by multiplying the number of letters in the name of a person by 2 such as follows:

Molly O' Brien

Number of letters $= 11$

Multiply by $2 = 2 \times 11 = 22$

Similarly, Roberto Montgomery has 17 letters and $17 \times 2 = 34$

So, we have, number of letters in the name Ahmad Adziz $= 10$

and $10 \times 2 = 20$

So, Ahmad Adziz would have 20 pleezorns.

59. Let x be the original fraction.

Then, according to the statement,

$$\left(3 \times \frac{1}{4}x\right) \times x = \frac{1}{12}$$

$$\Rightarrow \qquad \frac{3}{4}x^2 = \frac{1}{12}$$

$$\Rightarrow \qquad x^2 = \frac{1}{9}$$

$$\Rightarrow \qquad x = \frac{1}{3}$$

Hence, $\frac{1}{3}$ is the original fraction.

60. Given that,

'→' stands for '+'.

'←' stands for '–'.

'↑' stands for '÷'

'↓' stands for '×'.

' ' stands for '='.

So, $2 \downarrow 5 \leftarrow 6 \rightarrow 2 \uparrow 6 \quad 1$ is equal to $2 \times 5 - 6 + 2 \div 6 = 1$

$$= 10 - 6 + \frac{1}{3} = 4 + \frac{1}{3} = \frac{13}{3} \neq 1$$

Here, left hand side is not equal to right hand side, so the calculation done is not correct.

61. The figure in column (3) is the figure which is common to columns (1) and (2)

such as  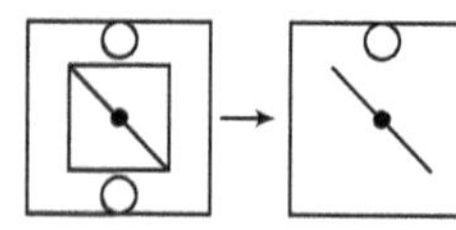

Similarly, 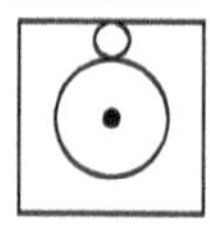 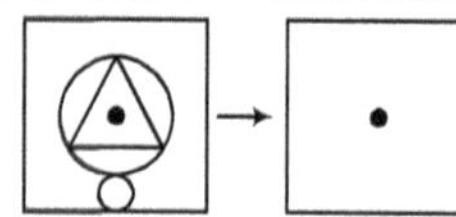

So,  is the correct figure for column (3).

62. This can be solved through following steps:

I. Two days before Saturday is Thursday.

II. The day immediately following Thursday is Friday.

III. Four days before Friday is Monday.

IV. Two days after Monday is Wednesday.

So, Wednesday is the correct answer.

63. Let Arthur takes x days to complete a work.

Then, Bert will take $\frac{2}{3}x$ days to complete the same work.

So, work done by Arthur in 1 day is $\frac{1}{x}$.

and work done by Bert in 1 day is $\frac{3}{2x}$.

Total work done by both in 1 day is $\frac{1}{24}$.

So, we have

$$\frac{1}{x}+\frac{3}{2x}=\frac{1}{24}$$

$$\Rightarrow \quad \frac{2+3}{2x}=\frac{1}{24}$$

$$\Rightarrow \quad \frac{5}{2x}=\frac{1}{24}$$

$$\Rightarrow \quad x=60$$

So, Arthur takes 60 days, whereas Bert takes $\frac{2}{3}\times 60 = 40$ days

64. Let the number of lions be x and number of eagles be y.

Now, total number of heads = 30

$$\Rightarrow \quad x+y=30 \quad \text{... (i)}$$

Also, number of legs = 86

$$\Rightarrow \quad 4x+2y=86 \quad \text{... (ii)}$$

Since, lions have four legs and eagles have two legs.

On solving Eqs. (i) and (ii), we get

$$\begin{aligned} 4x+4y &= 120 \\ 4x+2y &= 86 \\ - \quad - \quad & \quad - \\ \hline 2y &= 34 \\ \hline \end{aligned}$$

$$\Rightarrow \quad y=17$$

So, the number of eagles is 17 and number of lions = 30 − 17 = 13.

65. I returned on Tuesday.

Given, today is Friday.

Then, tomorrow is Saturday.

Now, day before Saturday is again Friday.

Day after Friday is Saturday, then four days before Saturday is Tuesday.

Hence, I returned on Tuesday from the trip.

66. In order to erect, the lamppost such that all roads must be lighted at the same time we need to erect lamppost at those points, which are connected to maximum number of roads.

Points connected to one road are 6 and 1.

Points connected to two roads are 3 and 5.

Points connected to three roads are 4 and 2.

Points connected to four roads are none.

So, lamppost must be connected to points 2 and 4, so that all roads are lighted.

67. Given, percentage of students taking English $= 64 = P(A)$

Percentage of students taking foreign language $= 22 = P(B)$

and percentage of students taking both $= 7 = P(A \cap B)$

Now, $P(A \cup B) = P(A) + P(B) - P(A \cap B)$

$= 64 + 22 - 7$

$= 79\%$

$\therefore$ Percentage of students who are taking neither subjects

$= (100 - 79)\%$

$= 21\%$

68. According to the net of the cube,

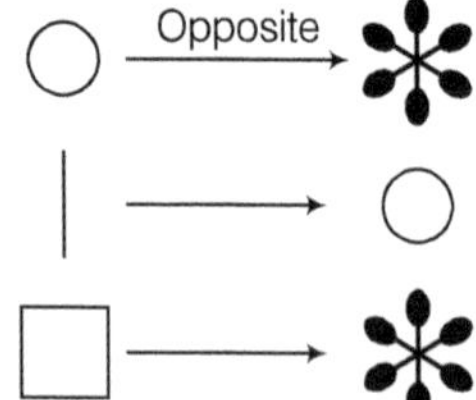

The different views of the cube

So, option (c) is incorrect view of the cube.

69. Let the number be x.

Taking half of it and adding one more, we get

$$\frac{x}{2}+1$$

Tripling it and adding four, we get

$$3\left(\frac{x}{2}+1\right)+4$$

This is equal to the number added to 23.

So, we have

$$3\left(\frac{x}{2}+1\right)+4=x+23$$

$$\Rightarrow \quad \frac{3}{2}x+3+4=x+23$$

$$\Rightarrow \quad \frac{x}{2}=16$$

$$\Rightarrow \quad x=32$$

Hence, the number is 32.

70. According to the given information,

Alice + Barbara $= A + B = 76$ ...(i)

Alice + Chloe ...(ii)

Barbara + Chloe $= B + C = 140$ ...(iii)

From Eqs. (i) and (ii), we have

$$C - B = 20 \quad \text{...(iv)}$$

From Eqs. (iii) and (iv), we have

$$2C = 160$$

$$\Rightarrow \quad C = 80$$

So, Chloe is 80 yr old.

Also, $\quad B + C = 140$

$$\Rightarrow \quad B = 140 - 80 = 60$$

So, Barbara is 60 yr old and hence Alice is (76 – 60) i.e. 16 yr old.

∴ Alice < Barbara < Chloe

Hence, the magician calls Alice to play his tricks.

71. The hands of the clock follows a pattern as follows:

(A) Hour hand : It moves three hours forward at each step.

(B) Minute hand : It moves 10 min backward at each step.

I	II	III	IV
1:30	4:20	7:10	10:00

So, the fourth clock face will show 10 O'clock as time.

72. There is a sequence occurring from the right eye to the left eye (as we look at them). Look at stages one and two. The contents of the eyes in stage one have merged to form the left eye of stage two and a new symbol has been introduced in the right eye of stage two. Now, look at stages two and three. The contents of the left eye in stage two has moved away and does not appear in stage three. The symbol from the right eye in stage two has moved to fill the left eye of stage three and a new symbol has been introduced in the right eye of stage three. This pattern of change is then continued, so that the left eye of stage four contains a merging of both eyes in stage three.
So, the pattern in sixth eye will have left eye as merging of both eyes in figure 5 and a new right eye. Hence, option (d) is correct.

73. Let we ate x idlis on the first day. Now according to the question,

Day	**Number of idlis eaten**
1st day	x
2nd day	$x + 6$
3rd day	$x + 12$
4th day	$x + 18$
5th day	$x + 24$
Total	$5x + 60$

$$\Rightarrow \quad 5x + 60 = 100$$

$$\therefore \quad x = 8$$

From the above, it is clear that he ate $x + 18 = 8 + 18 = 26$ idlis on the fourth day.

74. Area of the sheet of plywood available $= 3 \text{ ft} \times 8 \text{ ft} = 24 \text{ sq ft}$

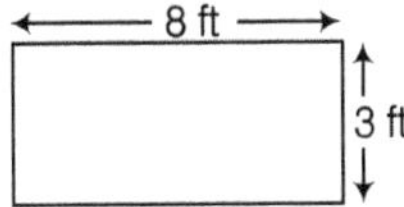

Area of the opening to be covered $= 2 \text{ ft} \times 12 \text{ ft} = 24 \text{ sq ft}$

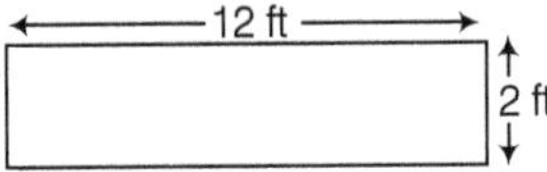

Since, the area of plywood and the area of the opening is equal, so it is possible to cover it completely.

Cut the board as indicated in Fig. 1 and shift the two pieces around as shown in Fig. 2. Hiram could now cover the hole perfectly.

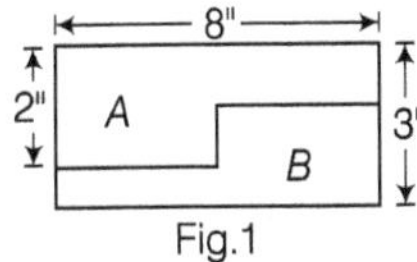

Fig.1

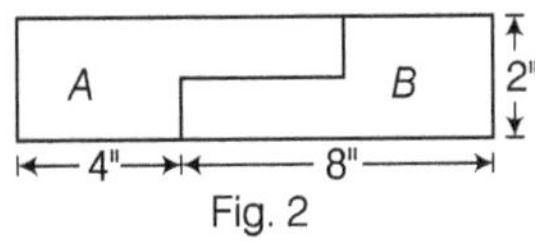

Fig. 2

75. In the first stage, the bottom horizontal line is removed from figure one and the bottom right vertical line in second figure is added to obtain the figure of second stage.

In the similar way, in third stage, the bottom horizontal line of figure one is removed and the bottom right vertical line in second figure is added to obtain the figure of stage 4.

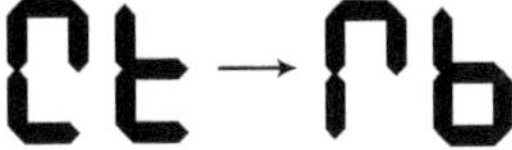

Hence, option (b) is correct.

76. Let us assume the number who complained about food only be x.

By Venn diagram,

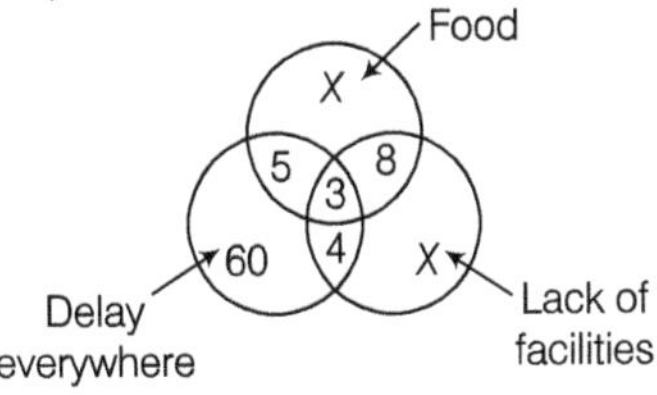

Those with complaints $= 400 - 240 = 160$

$\therefore \; x + x + 3 + 4 + 5 + 8 + 60 = 160 \quad \Rightarrow \quad 2x + 80 = 160$

$\Rightarrow \quad 2x = 80 \quad \Rightarrow \quad x = 40$

77. The mark on the ticket belonged to the game number (b), which has the figure (X) embedded in it.

Hence, option (b) is correct.

78. Total of all the numbers in each circle is equal to 100, so the missing number $= 100 - (9 + 20 + 4 + 8 + 2 + 16 + 31)$

$$= 100 - 90 = 10$$

So, question mark (?) will be replaced by 10.

79. The vacation was 20 days long. We can have rainy mornings followed by clear afternoons, clear mornings followed by rainy afternoons, or clear mornings followed by clear afternoons, we just can't have any totally rainy days.

Let M represents the number of rainy mornings. Then, the total number of mornings in the trip was $12 + M$. Let A represents the number of rainy afternoons. The total number of afternoons was $13 + A$. Since, the number of mornings in the trip is equal to the number of afternoons in the trip, we have $12 + M = 13 + A$

$$M - A = 1$$

There are no totally rainy days, and it rained on 15 days, so $M + A = 15$.

Solving the system of equations, we have $M = 8$ and $A = 7$. The vacation was $12 + 8 = 20$ days long.

80. The petal belonged to the Amazon flower (c).

Hence, option (c) is correct.

81. All the options, except option (b) have curved outer figure, whereas option (b) has straight line segments in the outer figure.

82. Evaluating the number of sections each student formed, we get

	Fig. 1	**Fig. 2**	**Fig. 3**	**Fig. 4**
Student 1	3	3	3	3
Student 2	2	3	5	4
Student 3	4	3	5	6
Student 4	3	4	6	8

So, student 4 has followed the rule correctly.

83. The powers of 7 have a repeating pattern for the last digit that can be found easily without performing the entire multiplication of each power.

7^0	7^1	7^2	7^3	7^4	7^5	7^6	7^7
1	7	9	3	1	7	9	3

So, 7^4 has units digit equal to 1.

Now, a number having units digit equal to 1 will always have units digit as 1 no matter what the power is.

Consider $7^{33} = 7^{32} \cdot 7^1 = (7^4)^8 \cdot 7^1$

So, $(7^4)^8$ will have units digit equal to 1.

Hence, $(7^4)^8 \times 7$ will have units digit equal to 7.

84. The illustration shows which five rods are removed. When these are removed, five equal triangles are left.

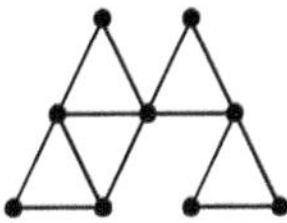

85. Total number of players $= 24 + 8 = 32$

Number of players to be on field at a time $= 24$

Duration of game $= 50$ min

$\therefore$ Duration of time for which each player would on field

$$= \frac{50 \times 24}{32} = 37.5 \text{ min}$$

86. Let the cost of one magazine be ₹x and the cost of one newspaper be ₹y.

Then, total cost of two copies of magazine and five copies of newspaper $= 2x + 5y$

We have, $2x + 5y = 15$ ...(i)

and also, $5x + 2y = 18.60$ ...(ii)

On solving Eqs. (i) and (ii), we get

$$\begin{array}{r} 10x + 25y = 75 \\ \underset{-}{10x} \underset{-}{+} 4y = \underset{-}{37.2} \\ \hline 21y = 37.8 \\ \hline \end{array}$$

$\Rightarrow$ $y =$ ₹1.8 and $x =$ ₹3

So, the cost of one magazine is ₹ 3.00 and the cost of one newspaper is ₹1.80.

87. The best way is to put one black pearl in the first vases and all other pearls in the second vase. Then, the probability of grabbing a black pearl from the first vase is 1 and the probability of grabbing a black pearl from the second vase is $\frac{99}{199}$.

$\therefore$ Total probability of grabbing a black pearl

$$=0.5\times1+0.5\times\frac{99}{199}=\frac{298}{398} \text{ (approx. 74.9\%)}.$$

88. Given, total number of children $=504$

and ratio of girls and boys $=5:3$

So, number of girls $=\frac{5}{8}\times504=5\times63=315$

Number of girls who participated in dance = 20% of 315

$$=\frac{20\times315}{100}=63$$

$\therefore$ Number of girls participated in solo song, group song and drama $=315-63=252$

Number of girls participated in group song and drama together

$$\frac{7}{9}\times252=196$$

89. There are 28 club members who have tried cauliflower and 19 who have tried spinach, for an apparent total of 47. But the 15 who have tried both cauliflower and spinach are counted twice in this total, eliminating that duplication gives a total of 32 members who have tried either cauliflower or spinach. That leaves $100-32=68$ members who have not tried either one. The club members break down can be given as follows :

68 have never tried cauliflower or spinach.

4 have tried spinach only.

13 have tried cauliflower only.

15 have tried both spinach and cauliflower.

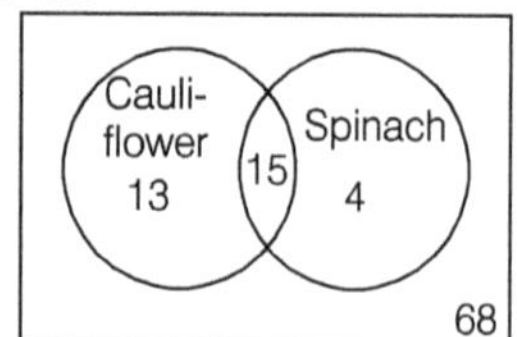

90. The wave pattern belonged to figure (d) of cyclonic waves.

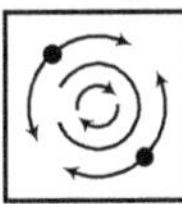

91. Consider the given numbers,

$$16 = 4^2$$
$$36 = 6^2$$
$$64 = 8^2$$
$$27 = 3^3$$
$$81 = 9^2$$

So, 27 is the odd one as it is the only number which is a cube of some numbers, other numbers are squares of some numbers.

92. Each figure except figure (a) has a pair which is the rotated form of circles, clockwise with the angle of rotation equal to 90°.

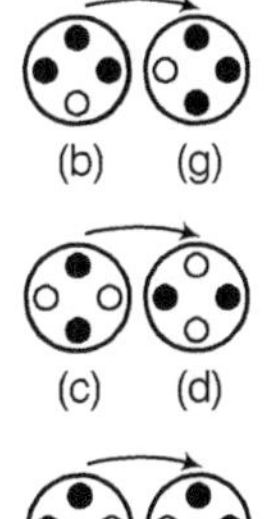

So, only figure (a) is left out having no pair.

93. The figure can be named as follows:

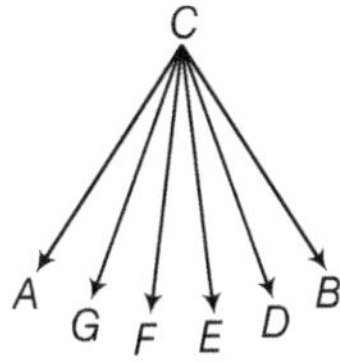

Number of angles with one element = 5

Number of angles with two elements = 4

Number of angles with three elements = 3

Number of angles with four elements = 2

Number of angles with five elements = 1

So, total number of angles = 5 + 4 + 3 + 2 + 1 = 15

94. From the given net of the cube, we have following cubes formed:

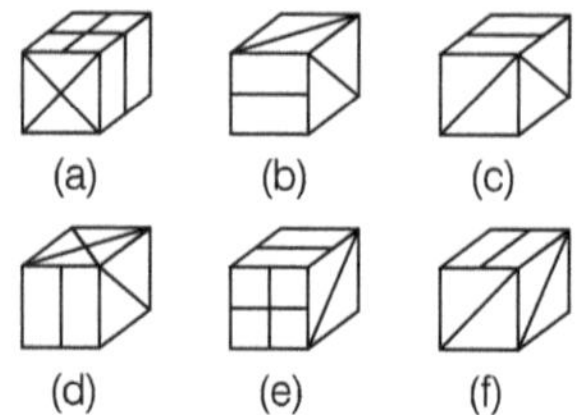

So, the figures (c) and (e) are not correct in the problem.

95. Here, the numbers are in pairs where the four-digit number is reversed and the largest digit is removed to form a three-digit number as follows:

$$5893 \rightarrow 385$$
$$6741 \rightarrow 146$$
$$2836 \rightarrow 632$$
$$5163 \rightarrow 315$$

Only number 983 is left alone with no pair, so it is the odd one.

96. The 'Swastik' is inscribed in the holy symbol (c) as shown below.

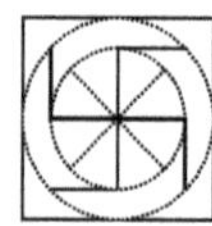

Hence, option (c) is correct.

97. The given number is

$$x = 0.7128888....$$

$$\Rightarrow \quad x = 0.712\overline{8}$$

Multiply both sides by 1000, we get

$$1000x = 712.\overline{8} \quad ...(i)$$

Again multiply both sides by 10, we get

$$10000x = 7128.\overline{8} \quad ...(ii)$$

On subtracting Eq. (i) from Eq. (ii), we get

$$9000x = 6416$$

$$\Rightarrow \quad x = \frac{6416}{9000}$$

$$= \frac{802}{1125}$$

98. Each successive number is the sum of the previous number and its reverse, as follows:

$$163 + 361 = 524$$
$$524 + 425 = 949$$
$$949 + 949 = 1898$$
$$1898 + 8981 = \boxed{10879}$$

Therefore, the missing number is 10879.

99. In this progression, each bag contains fewer coins than the preceding bag. Each bag contains a specific fraction of the number of coins in the first bag, which contains 60 coins, the pattern is as follows:

Bag (a) = 60 coins

Bag (b) = 30 coins (1/2)

Bag (c) = 20 coins (1/3)

Bag (d) = 15 coins (1/4)

Bag (e) = 12 coins (1/5)

Bag (f) = 10 coins (1/6)

100. The exact time of getting can be obtained by finding the mirror image of the time seen, i.e.

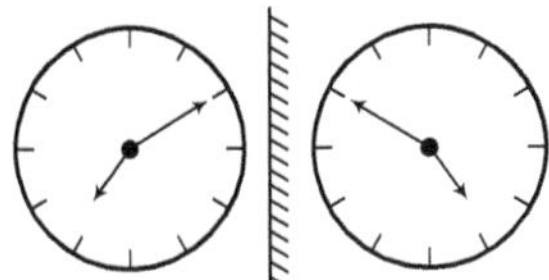

So, the time when the person woke was 4:50 am.

101. From the given information about the books, we can make the following table:

Hours	1	2	3	4	5	6
Books	MAT	UPSC	Lunch break session	CAT	Bank PO	CDS

From the statements given in question, the table will be formed as shown above, so we can easily find that the lunch break session must be in 3rd hour.

102. Let Jim's age be x yr. Then, Alf's age be $1.5x$ yr.

$\therefore$ Sid's age be $2.25x$ yr.

Given, total of their ages is 133.

According to the question,

$$x + 1.5x + 2.25x = 133$$

$$\Rightarrow \quad 4.75x = 133 \quad \Rightarrow \quad x = 28$$

So, the age of jim is 28 yr, the age of Alf is 42 yr and the age of Sid is 63 yr.

103 Given, Jasper's share = ₹ 3600

Now, Albert's share 20% more than Jaspher $= \frac{120}{100}$ of Jaspher's share

$$= \frac{120}{100} \times 3600 = 4320$$

Also, Albert's share is 25% more than Cyril

$$\Rightarrow \quad 4320 = \frac{125}{100} \text{ of } x \qquad \text{[Cyril's share]}$$

$$\Rightarrow \quad \frac{4320 \times 100}{125} = x$$

$$\Rightarrow \quad x = ₹3456$$

So, Cyril's share is ₹3456.

104. Younger daughter received more (4000 more) than elder daughter which is shown below:

Share of wife $= \frac{1}{3}$

Share of son $= \frac{1}{5}$

Share of elder daughter $= \frac{1}{6}$

Now, share of younger daughter $= 1 - \left(\frac{1}{3} + \frac{1}{5} + \frac{1}{6}\right) = 1 - \left(\frac{10 + 6 + 5}{30}\right)$

$$= 1 - \frac{21}{30} = \frac{9}{30} = \frac{3}{10}$$

Let the total estate be ₹x.

Then, younger daughter's share $= \frac{3}{10}x = 9000 \Rightarrow x =$ ₹ 30000

and elder daughter's share $= \frac{1}{6} \times 30000 =$ ₹ 5000

Therefore, younger daughter's share is more than elder daughter's share.

105. The different codes used for letters are as follow

R ⟶ N
D ⟶ T
I ⟶ U
O ⟶ I
E ⟶ R
T ⟶ O
U ⟶ D
N ⟶ C
C ⟶ E

So, the word 'INTRODUCE' in panel's language will be

I N T R O D U C E
↓ ↓ ↓ ↓ ↓ ↓ ↓ ↓ ↓
U C O N I T D E R

106. The puzzle can be solved through following steps:

Clue 1. The middle numbers add up to 5.

i.e. the middle number can (3, 2), (2, 3), (4, 1), (1, 4).

Clue 2. 4 is to the left of but next to the 1.

i.e. 4 and 1 are together such that pair (4, 1) is formed.

⇒ Middle number will be (4, 1) as the sum of middle numbers must be 5 and 4 must be left to 1.

Clue 3. The number on far rights is bigger than on the far left.

i.e. the number of far right is 3 and on far left is 2.

So, the solution to the puzzle is | 2 | 4 | 1 | 3 |.

107. There are five sections of a circle which are equal in size, so a regular pentagon will be formed when these parts will be assembled systematical, as given below:

108. At each stage, the top left hand line is moving through half the length of one side clockwise.

Hence, option (b) is correct.

109. In Ruppert's puzzle, the four given numbers 2, 3, 4 and 5 with signs of '+' and '=' are to be arranged in such a way that makes a sensible equation.

One of the possibilities is $2+5=7$ and $4+3=7$

but here two '+' signs are required.

So, one of the ways to represent a sensible equation using above numbers and signs is $3^2=4+5$

where, $3^2=9$ and $4+5=9$

So, $3^2=4+5$ makes a correct equation.

110. Let my sister's present age be x yr and my age be y yr.

According to the problem,

$$y=x+10 \quad \text{...(i)}$$

Also, my age after one year will be $(y+1)$ yr and my sister's age after one year will be $(x+1)$ yr.

$$\therefore \quad (y+1)=2(x+1)$$

$$\Rightarrow \quad y+1=2x+2$$

$$\Rightarrow \quad y=2x+1 \quad \text{...(ii)}$$

On solving Eqs. (i) and (ii), we get

$$0=-x+9 \Rightarrow x=9$$

So, $$y=9+10=19$$

$\therefore$ Present age of my sister is 9 yr and my present age is 19 yr.

Now, let z years before, I was three times as old as my sister.

We have, $(19-z)=3(9-z)$

$$\Rightarrow \quad 19-z=27-3z$$

$$\Rightarrow \quad 2z=8 \Rightarrow z=4$$

So, 4 yr before, I was 3 times as old as my sister.

111. Here, the place value of letters are being used to find the result.

The problem is as follows:

$$\frac{\text{ABC}}{3}=\text{DA} \Rightarrow \frac{123}{3}=41=\text{DA}$$

$$\frac{\text{DEF}}{6}=\text{GF} \Rightarrow \frac{456}{6}=76=\text{GF}$$

$$\frac{\text{GHI}}{3}=\text{ZC} \Rightarrow \frac{789}{3}=\underline{26}3=\text{ZC}$$

According to above pattern,

$$\frac{\text{FGH}}{6}=\frac{678}{6}=1\underline{1}3=\text{KC}$$

Hence, option (c) is correct.

112. The dogs' numbers are decided on the basis of the sum of the values of the letters in their name where each consonant $=1$

and each vowel = 4.

The pattern is as follows:

Corgi $= c + o + r + g + i = 1 + 4 + 1 + 1 + 4 = 11$

Alsatian $= 4 + 1 + 1 + 4 + 1 + 4 + 4 + 1 = 20$

Terrier $= 1 + 4 + 1 + 1 + 4 + 4 + 1 = 16$

$\therefore$ Wolfhound $= 1 + 4 + 1 + 1 + 1 + 4 + 4 + 1 + 1 = 18$

Hence, wolfhound number is 18.

113. The model is 8000000 times lighter than the real Eiffel Tower. Both are made of the same metal, and so the volume of the model should be 8000000 times less than that of the real tower.

We know that, the volumes of similar figures are to one another as the cubes of their altitudes.

Therefore, the model must be 200 times smaller than the original, because $200 \times 200 \times 200 = 8000000$.

The altitude of the real tower is 300 m and so the height of the model should be 300 : 200 = 3/2 m = 1.5 m.

Then, the model will be about the height of a man.

114. The railway installed the system in series that can be divided into 5 groups of 3 terms each, each group comprising of 2 letters followed by number.

Z_25 / YB 23 / XC_ / W_19 / _E17

Observing the group Y B 23, we find that in a group, the number is the difference of the numbers representing the positions of the 2 letters in the English alphabet.

Thus, putting $=1$, $=2, \ldots,$ $=25$, $=26$

We have, $B = 25 - 2 = 23$

Similarly, missing term in 3rd group = $C = 24 - 3 = 21$

Missing term in 1st group = $- 25 = 26 - 25 = 1 =$

Missing term in 4th group $- 19 = 23 - 19 = 4 =$

and missing term in 5th group $+ 17 = 5 + 17 = 22 = V$

So, the complete sequence is Z A 25 Y B 23 X C 21 W D 19 V E 17.

115. Total number of passengers in train A $= 700$ [given]

Total number of passengers in train B

$$= \frac{130 \times 700}{100} = 910$$

In train A,

Total number of passengers in General coach = 20% of 700

$$= \frac{20 \times 700}{100} = 140$$

Now, given that one-fourth of the total number of passengers of train A are in AC coach.

So, the number of passengers in AC coach in train A

$$= \frac{1}{4} \times 700 = 175$$

Given that, total number of passengers in AC coach in both the trains together is 480.

Let total number of passengers of train B in AC coach $= x$

Then, $480 = 175 + x$

$\Rightarrow$ $x = 305$

So, total number of passengers in the general coach of train A and the AC coach of train B together $= 305 + 140 = 445$

116. Using the correct symbols given as

$$P \longrightarrow \div$$
$$Q \longrightarrow \times$$
$$R \longrightarrow +$$
$$S \longrightarrow -$$

We have the expression as 18 Q 12 P 4 R 5 S 6

$$= 18 \times 12 \div 4 + 5 - 6$$
$$= 18 \times 3 + 5 - 6$$
$$= 54 + 5 - 6$$ [using BODMAS rule]
$$= 59 - 6 = 53$$

117. There are infinite number of such numbers. The difference between divisor and remainder is always 2.

i.e. $(3-1) = 2, (4-2) = 2, (5-3) = 2, (6-4) = 2$

Then, 2 plus the desired number is a multiple of the divisors given.

Lowest common multiple of 3, 4, 5 and 6 = LCM (3, 4, 5, 6) $= 60$

Then, the desired number $= 60 - 2 = 58$

118. The different symbols used by the mathematician to denote the operations are

$$> \longrightarrow `+'$$
$$< \longrightarrow `-'$$
$$+ \longrightarrow `\div'$$
$$\wedge \longrightarrow `\times'$$
$$- \longrightarrow `='$$
$$\times \longrightarrow `>'$$
$$= \longrightarrow `<'$$

Now, consider

$$8 < 4 + 2 = 6 > 3$$
$$= 8 - 4 \div 2 < 6 + 3$$
$$= 8 - 2 < 9$$
$$= 6 < 9$$

It is true.

Hence, option (c) follows the symbols correctly.

119. The six 4's can be arranged in the following way to get 100 :

$$4 \times [(4 \times 4) + 4 + 4] + 4$$
$$= 4 \times [16 + 4 + 4] + 4$$
$$= 4 \times [24] + 4$$
$$= 96 + 4 = 100$$

120. A fair division of the coins is indeed possible. Let the number of rooms be N. This means that per room there are N chests with N coins each. In total, there are $N \times N \times N = N^3$ coins. One chest with N coins goes to the barber. For the six brothers, $N^3 - N$ coins remain.

We can write this as : $N(N^2 - 1)$ or $N(N - 1)(N + 1)$. This last expression is divisible by 6 in all cases, since a number is divisible by 6 when it is both divisible by 3 and even. This is indeed the case here : whatever N may be, the expression $N(N - 1)(N + 1)$ always contains three successive numbers. One of those is always divisible by 3, and atleast one of the others is even. This even holds when $N = 1$; in that case all the brothers get nothing, which is also a fair division.

121. As per the statements,

Kaf navcki roi $\xrightarrow{\text{means}}$ Take three pieces ...(i)

Kir roi palt ⟶ Hide three coins ...(ii)

Inoti kaf kir ⟶ Cautiously take coins ...(iii)

From statements (i) and (ii), Roi means three.

From statements (ii) and (iii), Kir means coins.

∴ Palt means hide.

Also, from statements (i) and (iii), Kaf means take.

∴ Inoti means cautiously and navcki means pieces.

∴ 'Hide pieces cautiously' stands for 'Palt navcki inoti'.

122. Distance travelled by me $= 60$ mph $\times 4 = 240$ miles

Average of the vehicle = 40 miles per gallon

∴ Petrol used by the vehicle in travelling 240 miles $= \frac{240}{40} = 6$ gallons

Total petrol in tank = 10 gallons

So, petrol got wasted $= 10 - 6 = 4$ gallons

123. Let

- x denotes the number of days we jogged in the morning and stayed at home in the evening.
- y denotes the number of days we played tennis in the evening and did nothing in the morning.
- z denotes the number of days we neither jogged nor played tennis.

Then,

$y + z =$ Number of mornings we did nothing $= 12$

$x + z =$ Number of evenings we stayed at home $= 12$

$x + y =$ Number of days we jogged or played tennis $= 10$

Adding the above three equations and dividing both sides by 2 gives

$$x + y + z = 17$$

Since, there are only three types of days, the total number of days 1 stayed with my cousin is their sum. i.e. 17.

124. As per the rule given, following symbols will be transferred.

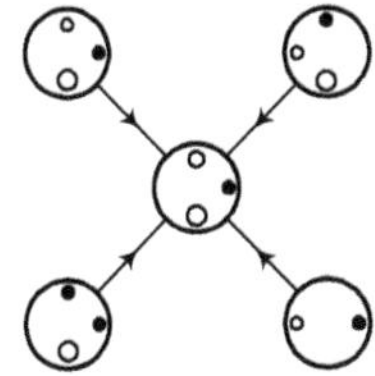

1. As the upper circle 'O' is repeated once only.
2. As the lower circle 'O' is repeated thrice.
3. The dot '•' on the right is repeated thrice.

Hence, option (d) is correct.

125. *True*

Because there must be one or the other.

126. The centre point of the area where the five friends stay will be the correct meeting point to reduce the walking time to minimum.

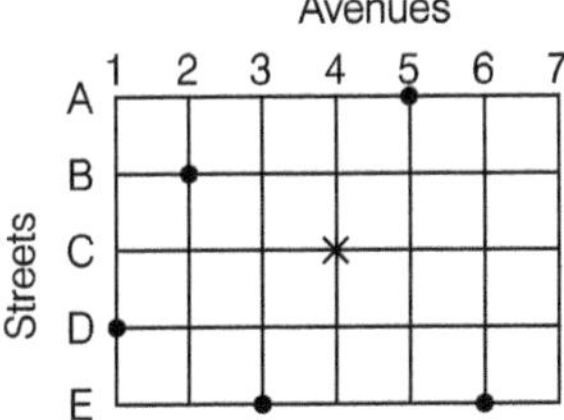

The centre point of streets A, B, C, D and E is street C.

The centre point of avenues 1, 2, 3, 4, 5, 6, 7 is 4.

Hence, point C 4 will be the correct meeting point.

127. Let the time passed be x and the time to come be y.

Then, $$x + y = 99 \quad \text{...(i)}$$

Also, $$\frac{2}{3}x = \frac{4}{5}y$$

$$\Rightarrow \quad \frac{x}{y} = \frac{4}{5} \times \frac{3}{2}$$

$$\Rightarrow \quad \frac{x}{y} = \frac{6}{5}$$

$$\Rightarrow \quad y = \frac{5}{6}x \quad \text{...(ii)}$$

From Eqs. (i) and (ii), we get

$$x + \frac{5}{6}x = 99$$

$$\Rightarrow \quad \frac{6x + 5x}{6} = 99$$

$$\Rightarrow \quad \frac{11}{6}x = 99$$

$$\Rightarrow \quad x = 54$$

Hence, 54 yr has passed.

128. Let the first system be X and second system be Y.

Then,

X	Y
14	36
133	87

In order to get an idea of some relationship between the two systems, we will subtract 14 from 133 as,

$$133 - 14 = 119$$

and compare that to the difference of 87 and 36 as,

$$87 - 36 = 51$$

We can compare 119 to 51, but first, let's reduce it on dividing by 17, gives us 7 to 3.

So, it is clear that for every 7° on the X thermometer, Y will increase or decrease by 3°. When X is at 14, if we move towards X making it 0° $(14 - 7 \times 2)$, Y will be reduced by 6° (3×2). So, Y will show 30°.

When X is 0°, Y is 30°, giving us the formula $Y = \frac{3}{7}X + 30$.

To find the temperature at which both thermometers read the same, set Y equal to X, and the formula then becomes

$$X = \frac{3}{7}X + 30$$

$$\Rightarrow \quad \frac{4}{7}X = 30$$

$$\Rightarrow \quad 4X = 210$$

$$\therefore \quad X = 52.5^\circ$$

129. It is impossible to average 60 mph for this trip. At 30 mph, the car would travel 1 mile in 2 min; at 60 mph, the car would travel 2 miles in 2 min. So, in order to average 60 mph, the entire trip of 2 miles would have to be completed in 2 min. But the driver has already used 2 min going from point *A* to point *B*; there's no time left to get from point *B* to point *C*.

130. Time taken by father to accomplish the task alone is 12 h.

So, the work done by him in 1 h is $\frac{1}{12}$.

Time taken by both son and father to accomplish the task is 8 h.
Therefore, the work done by both in 1 h is $\frac{1}{8}$.

So, the work done by son alone in 1 h $= \frac{1}{8} - \frac{1}{12} = \frac{1}{24}$.

Therefore, the time taken by son to complete the task is 24 h.

131. Let us draw the passage followed by Ragini.

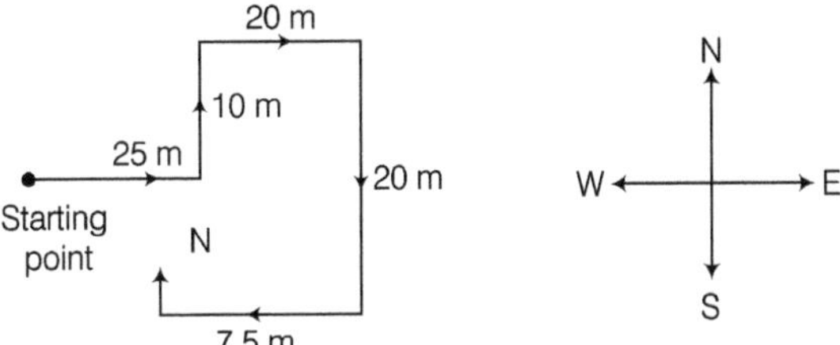

So, the direction in which Ragini is walking, is North.
Hence, option (c) is correct.

132. There are several method to solve this puzzle, one of which uses a chart comparing their movements. It helps to realise that the correct answer must involve whole number (not fractional) revolutions.

x (3 yr)	y (5 yr)
3 yr = 1 revolution	$\frac{3}{5}$ revolutions
6 yr = 2 revolutions	$\frac{6}{5}$ revolutions
9 yr = 3 revolutions	$\frac{9}{5}$ revolutions
12 yr = 4 revolutions	$\frac{12}{5}$ revolutions
15 yr = 5 revolutions	3 revolutions

So, in 15 yr, x and y will be exactly in line.

133. In each row, the third figure is formed by combining the first two figures as follows:

Similarly in row 3, we have

Hence, option (c) is correct.

134. Moving from top to bottom, double each number and subtract 1, 2, 3, 4 and 5 accordingly we get the final number.

So, the series move like this

$$53$$
$$\downarrow$$
$$53 \times 2 - 1 = 105$$
$$\downarrow$$
$$105 \times 2 - 2 = 208$$
$$\downarrow$$
$$208 \times 2 - 3 = 413$$
$$\downarrow$$
$$413 \times 2 - 4 = 822$$
$$\downarrow$$
$$822 \times 2 - 5 = 1639$$

So, the required number is 1639.

135. 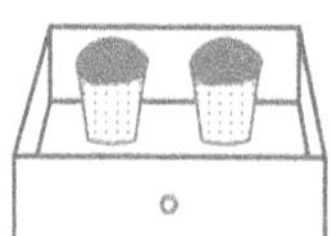 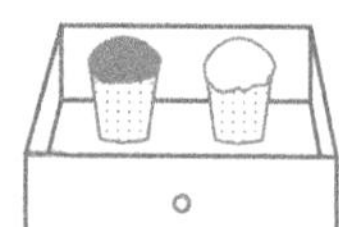 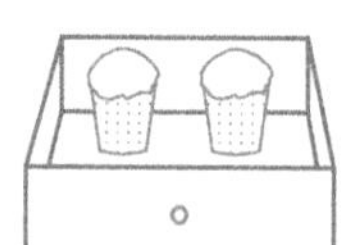

As you can see, there are only three possibilities, where a chocolate cupcake could be chosen first.

136. The number is such that when

Divided by 2 will give a remainder of 1.

Divided by 3 will give a remainder of 2.

Divided by 4 will give a remainder of 3.

Divided by 5 will give a remainder of 4.

Divided by 6 will give a remainder of 5.

Divided by 7 will give a remainder of 6.

Divided by 8 will give a remainder of 7.

Divided by 9 will give a remainder of 8.

Divided by 10 will give a remainder of 9.

Difference between divisor and remainder in each case is 1.

$(2-1), (3-2), (4-3), (5-4), (6-5),$

$(7-6), (8-7), (9-8)$ and $(10-9) = 1$

$\therefore$ Required number of stamps = LCM (2, 3, 4, 5, 6, 7, 8, 9, 10) −1

$= 2520 - 1 = 2519$

137. Let king of hearts is denoted by 'KH'.

Ace of spades is denoted by 'AS'.

Three of diamonds is denoted by 'TD'.

Nine of clubs is denoted by 'NC'.

By statement 1, we get

KH	AS

or

AS	KH

By statement 2, we get

KH	AS	TD

or

TD	AS	KH

By statement 3, we get

NC	KH	AS	TD

or

TD	AS	KH	NC

So, the king of hearts is next to nine of clubs.

138. Let the initial amount of diesel in each of the diesel tank be D.

Now, let us assume that they drove for H hours.

In that case, the amount of diesel used by William's truck in H hours $= \frac{D \times H}{4}$

The amount of diesel used by Johnson's truck $= \frac{D \times H}{5}$

Therefore, the diesel left in William's truck $= D - \frac{DH}{4}$

Diesel left in the Johnson's truck $= D - \frac{DH}{5}$

Now, according to the question,

$$D - \frac{DH}{5} = 4\left(D - \frac{DH}{4}\right)$$

$$\Rightarrow \quad \frac{5D - DH}{5} = 4\left(\frac{4D - DH}{4}\right)$$

$$\Rightarrow \quad H = \frac{15}{4} = 3\frac{3}{4}\text{ h}$$

139. In the operations done by participant 3, we get the expression as

$$700 \div 10 \times \frac{1}{2} + 35 - 70$$

$$= 70 \times \frac{1}{2} + 35 - 70$$

$$= 35 + 35 - 70 = 0$$

140. At the rate of ₹1 for ten weeks, we figure that the amount of interest for one year would be ₹5.20. But I do not have the use of my ₹10 for the entire period of time. But on the average just half that amount.

So, we conclude that I paid ₹5.20 to use ₹5 for one year.

i.e. $$\frac{5.2}{5} = \frac{104}{100} = 104\%$$

Hence, the annual rate of simple interest is 104%.

141. Consider the first number 16

Now, $16 + (1 + 6) = 16 + 7 = 23$

$23 + (2 + 3) = 23 + 5 = 28$

$28 + (2 + 8) = 28 + 10 = 38$

$38 + (3 + 8) = 38 + 11 = \boxed{49}$

So, the rule followed here is add the sum of the two digits of the number to the number itself which will give the number in next box.

142. The given hexagon solves the criteria that one dot is inside each of the figure, two squares and one circle and the other dot is inside two squares.

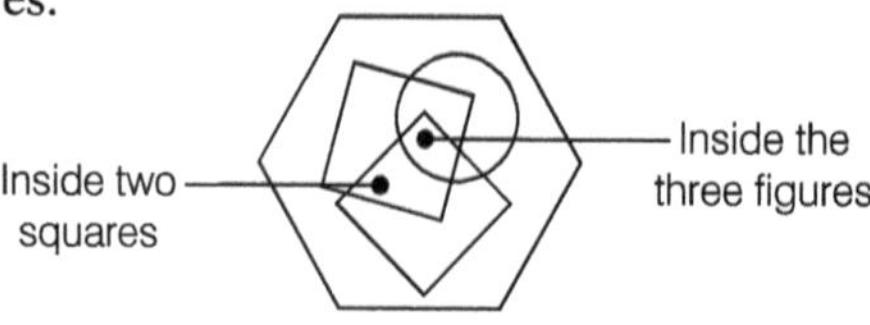

Now, if we had a dot in figure (c), then we will have the same relation as in the above figure.

Hence, option (c) is correct.

143. Here, point A is the actual destination and point B is where Mr. Dixit reached. Distance between point A and point B is 5 m. So, Mr. Dixit is 5 m away from his actual destination.

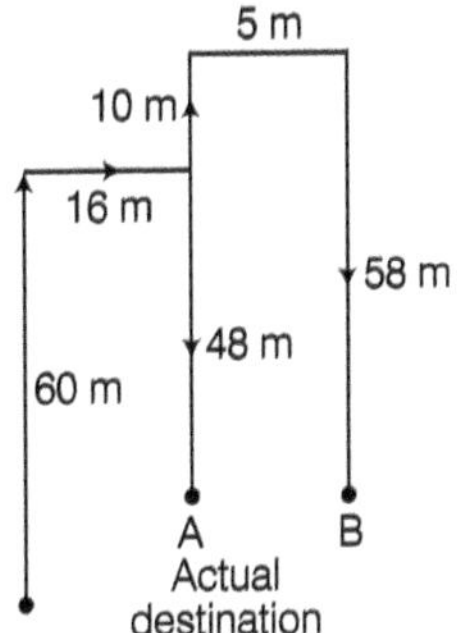

144. Let us arrange the given information as follows, where '✓' means on and '×' means off.

Lights / Waiters	1	2	3	4
Raman	✓	✓	✓	✓
Pawan	✓	✓	×	×
Rakesh	✓	×	×	×
Hitesh	×	✓	✓	✓
Mithlesh	×	×	✓	✓

Now, when lights two and three boths are off, it a signal for waiter Rakesh that his order is ready.

145. It only took John four steps to accomplish his task.

Step 1. John filled the five gallon bucket and poured all of it into the six gallon bucket.

Step 2. He refilled the five gallon bucket and poured out one gallon into the six gallon bucket to fill it, leaving four gallons in the five gallon bucket.

Step 3. He dumped the six gallon bucket and poured the four gallons from the five gallon bucket into the six gallon bucket.

Step 4. Then, John refilled the five gallon bucket and started home for a piece of cake.

146. The salami slices can be arranged in the given manner:

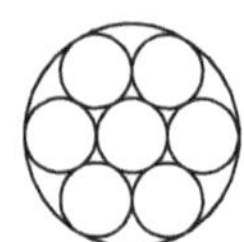

So, seven slices of salami can be arranged on the pizza dough without overlapping each other.

147. In the given figures, the pattern in the outer circle is repeated in the inner circle in all the figures except in figure (c).

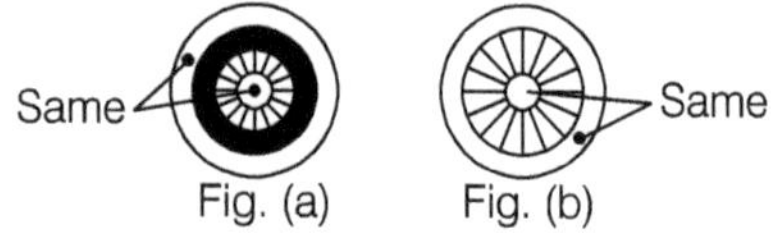

Fig. (a) Fig. (b)

But in figure (c),

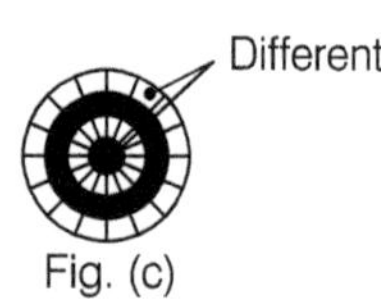

Fig. (c)

Hence, option (c) is correct.

148. Each shot has chance of 1/3 to be the best. This is because the result of a shot is not dependent on an earlier shot. The chance that the third shot is not the best shot is 1 minus the chance that the third shot is the best shot. Therefore, the answer is 2/3.

You can also look at the possible outcomes. Call the three successive arrows A, B and C. We know that, arrow B is further from the bull's eye than arrow A. So, after shooting arrow C, the following three outcomes are possible:

Best		Worse
A	B	C
A	C	B
C	A	B

For two of the three outcomes, arrow C is worse than arrow A.

149. The illustration requires no explanation. It shows clearly how the three circles may be drawn so that every cat has a separate enclosure and cannot approach another cat without crossing a line.

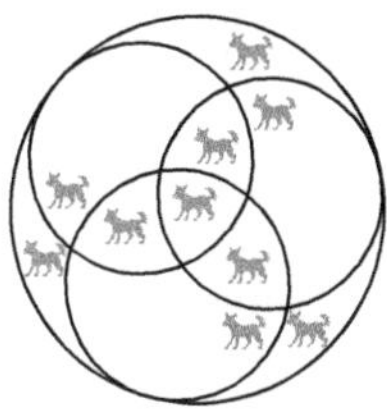

150. Let the price of the fourth item be ₹ x.

Then, total of the prices of four items $= 1.50 + 3.00 + 4.00 + x$

$= 8.50 + x$

and product of the prices of the four items $= (1.50)(3.00)(4.00)(x)$

$= 18x$

Since, the result of the above is same, so we have

$$8.50 + x = 18x$$

$$\Rightarrow \quad 8.50 = 17x$$

$$\Rightarrow \quad 0.50 = x$$

Therefore, the price of the fourth item is ₹ 0.50.

151. The waist size and the weight of Herman is increasing in a pattern and forming series as follows:

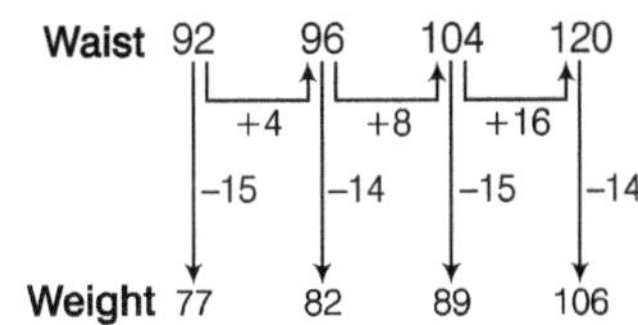

So, the weight of Herman at the age 50, having waist size 120 cm will be 106 kg.

152. **First option**

Initial salary = ₹ 40000

First year : (20000 + 20000) = 40000

Second year : (21000 + 21000) = 42000

Second option Initial salary = ₹ 40000

First year : (20000 + 20500) = 40500

Second year : (21000 + 21500) = 42500

So, option two is more beneficial for the employee.

153. Let the cost of egg alone be ₹ x.

Then, cost of the toy $= x + 4$

Given, total cost of the toy is ₹4.50.

So, $x + x + 4 = 4.50 \Rightarrow 2x = 0.50 \Rightarrow x =$ ₹ 0.25

Therefore, the cost of toy is ₹ $(0.25 + 4)$ i.e. ₹ 4.25.

154. Most people will think of is to use the fastest person as an usher to guide everyone across. How long would that take $10 + 1 + 7 + 1 + 2 = 21$ mins. Is that it ? No, because that would make this question too simple even as a warm up question.

Now, to reduce the amount of time, we should find a way for 10 and 7 to go together. If they cross together, then we need one of them to come back to get the others. That would not be ideal. How do we get around that? May be we can have 1 waiting on the other side to bring the torch back.

We are getting closer. The fastest way to get 1 across and be back is to use 2 to usher 1 across. So, let's put all this together.

Person went	Time clasped
1 and 2 cross	2 min
1 return	1 min
7 and 10 cross	10 min
2 return	2 min
1 and 2 cross	2 min
Total	17 min

155. Percentage of gum chewers $= 78\%$

People under the age of fifteen $= 35\%$

So, percentage of non-gum chewers $= 22\%$

and people above the age of fifteen $= 65\%$

$\therefore$ Probability of person chosen at random to be a non-gum chewer and above the age fifteen $= 22\% \times 65\% = 14.30$

156. Let the rate of the still water be 'a' and the rate of stream be 'b' mph.

When rowing towards downstream, then speed of Sara's boat will be $(a + b)$ mph $= 4$ mph and when rowing upstream against the stream, then speed of Sara's boat will be $(a - b)$ mph.

The distance rowed by her downstream $= 4 \times 2$ miles $= 8$ miles

Now, rowing back took her four hours covering distance of 8 miles with speed $(a - b)$ mph.

$$\therefore \qquad \frac{8}{a - b} = 4 \quad \Rightarrow \quad 2 = a - b$$

So, the rate of boat in still water is 3 mph and the rate of stream is 1 mph.

157. If each family that have three bicycles, give away one of their bicycles to those possessing only one bicycle, then each family in the village will have two bicycles.

Therefore, there are in total $29 \times 2 = 58$ bicycles in the village.

Alternate Method

We represented by a the number of families having one bicycle and by b those families who have two bicycles, while the number of families with three bicycles is also represented by a.

Now, $a + b + a = 29$ ...(i)

$\therefore$ Number of bicycles in the village

$$= 1 \times a + 2 \times b + 3 \times a = 4a + 2b = 2(a + b + a)$$
$$= 2 \times 29 \quad \text{[from Eq. (i)]}$$
$$= 58$$

Hence, there are 58 bicycles in the village.

158. I. The day which comes two days after Monday is Wednesday.

II. The day which comes immediately after Wednesday is Thursday.

III. The day which comes two days after Thursday is Saturday.

IV. The day which comes three days after Saturday is Tuesday.

So, Miss. Greg should guess Tuesday to attend the party.

159. The mirror image of the given figure is

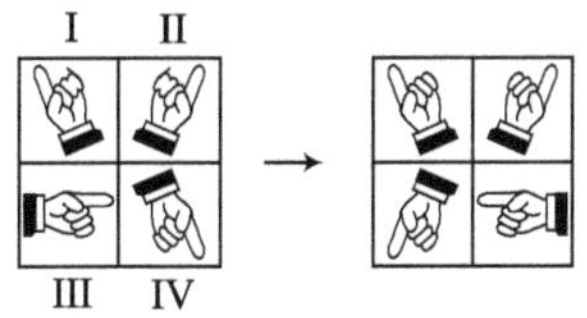

Here, figures I and II are interchanged and had a lateral inversion.

Similarly, figures III and IV are interchanged and laterally inverted.

Hence, option (a) is correct.

160. As per the example,

$$\underline{2}\ \underline{3}\ \underline{3}\ \underline{3}\ \underline{5}\ \underline{20} = + - \times \times (\ )(\ )$$
$$5 + (2 \times 3) = 20 - (3 \times 3) = 11$$

Using the same method, we have

$$\underline{2}\ \underline{3}\ \underline{6}\ \underline{8}\ \underline{8}\ \underline{16} = \times \times // (\ )(\ )$$

By hit and trial method, we have

$$(2 \times 6)/3 = (8 \times 8)/16$$

as $(2 \times 6)/3 = 12/3 = 4$

and $(8 \times 8)/16 = 64/16 = 4$

$\therefore$ LHS = RHS

161. The scheduled time to reach the station is 8:30 am.

When it met the engineer, it saved 10 min, 5 to get to the station and 5 to come back to the meeting point. Therefore, the engineer meet the car at 8:25 am.

In other words, if it saved 10 min that means half of the time was saved in meeting at a point and half in reaching the office, i.e. he met 5 min early at 8:25 am.

162. In the given square, each small square in the corner having four elements follows a pattern as follows:

The product of numbers on first row of square is equal to the number below:

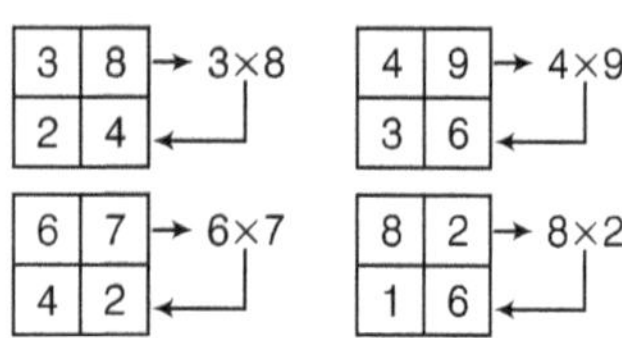

So, the missing number is 6.

163. The suitcase is divided into four parts in such a way that all the parts are of same size and shape though being the mirror image of each other as well.

164. The mirror image of the figure (X) will be image of the card which is as follows:

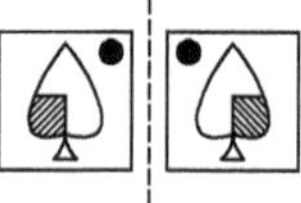

Here, figure (a) matches the image of the card.
Hence, option (a) is correct.

165. The given figure is

Rejoining the figures, so that the sides are aligned flatly and squarely, we get

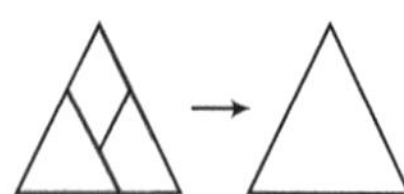

Therefore, a triangle is formed.
Hence, option (c) is correct.

166. The clues can be used to find the number as follows:

1. Since, the number is divisible by 3. So, the sum of the digits is a multiple of 3, i.e. 3, 6, 9.
2. Also, the sum of digits lies between 4 and 8, so the sum of digits must be 6.

   So, the combination can be 15, 24, 33, 42, 51.
3. But the number lies between 1-36. So, the options reduced to 15, 24, 33.
4. Also, the number is an odd number, so the options reduced to 15 and 33.
5. According to the last clue, the product of digits lies between 4 and 8, so 15 is the correct number as $3 \times 3 = 9$.

   Hence, 15 is the number, I bet on.

167. Using the sign for each participant, following results are obtained.

According to the Participant 1

'+' ⟶ '–'

'–' ⟶ '×'

'×' ⟶ '÷'

'÷' ⟶ '×'

So, $200 \times 100 + 300 \times 200 - 10 \div 2 + 40$

$= 200 \div 100 - 300 \div 200 \times 10 \times 2 - 40$

$= 2 - \frac{3}{2} \times 10 \times 2 - 40$

$= 2 - 30 - 40 = 2 - 70 = -68$

According to the Participant 2

'+' ⟶ '–'

'–' ⟶ '÷'

'×' ⟶ '+'

'÷' ⟶ '×'

So, $200 \times 100 + 300 \times 200 - 10 \div 2 + 40$

$= 200 + 100 - 300 + 200 \div 10 \times 2 - 40$

$= 200 + 100 - 300 + 20 \times 2 - 40$

$= 200 + 100 - 300 + 40 - 40 = 0$

According to the Participant 3

'+' ⟶ '×'

'–' ⟶ '–'

'×' ⟶ '+'

'÷' ⟶ '×'

So, $200 \times 100 + 300 \times 200 - 10 \div 2 + 40$

$$200 + 100 \times 300 + 200 - 10 \times 2 \times 40$$
$$= 200 + 30000 + 200 - 20 \times 40$$
$$= 400 + 30000 - 800 = 29600$$

According to the Participant 4

'×' ⟶ '–'

'+' ⟶ '÷'

'–' ⟶ '+'

'÷' ⟶ '×'

So, $200 \times 100 + 300 \times 200 - 10 \div 2 + 40$

$$= 200 - 100 \div 300 - 200 + 10 \times 2 \div 40$$
$$= 200 - \frac{1}{3} - 200 + 20 \div 40$$
$$= -\frac{1}{3} + \frac{1}{2} = \frac{3-2}{6} = \frac{1}{6}$$

So, the participant (2) has used the notation correctly to get the sum equal to 0.

168. To arrange the numbers in such a way that no two consecutive numbers are adjacent, horizontally, vertically or diagonally, following pattern can be used:

<table>
<tr><td rowspan="2">2</td><td>4</td><td>1</td><td>5</td><td rowspan="2">7</td></tr>
<tr><td>6</td><td>8</td><td>3</td></tr>
</table>

169. If postman Pat had delivered mail three times at each house, then the total sum of the house numbers per day would be $(1 + 2 + 3 + 4 + 5 + 6 + 7 + 8 + 9 + 10) \times 3 = 165$. Now, that sum is $18 + 12 + 23 + 19 + 32 + 25 = 129$. The difference is $165 - 129 = 36$; divided by 3 this is 12. The sum of the house numbers where no mail was delivered is therefore 12.

The following combinations are possible:

$$2 + 10$$
$$3 + 9$$
$$4 + 8$$
$$5 + 7$$

Each day, at four houses the mail was delivered. On Tuesday, the sum was 12. 12 can only be made from four house numbers in two ways:

$$1 + 2 + 3 + 6$$
$$1 + 2 + 4 + 5$$

The same holds for Friday with the sum of 32:

$$5 + 8 + 9 + 10$$
$$6 + 7 + 9 + 10$$

From this, we can conclude that the house numbers 1, 2, 9 and 10 for sure have received mail, which means that the combinations 2 + 10 and 3 + 9 are not possible. In addition, the combination 5 + 7 is not possible, because mail was delivered either at house 5 or at house 7. Thus, the only remaining solution is: houses 4 and 8.

170. The pattern for the given numbers is as follows:

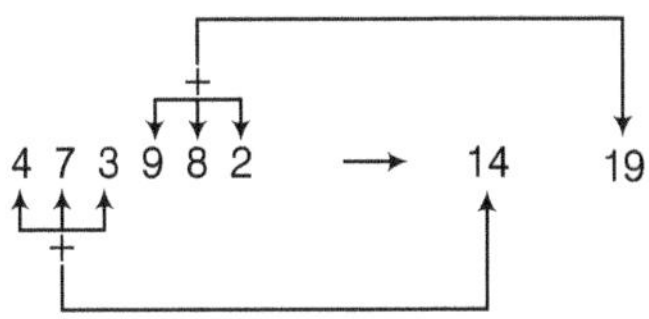

i.e. $4 + 7 + 3 = 14$ and $9 + 8 + 2 = 19$

Similarly, $329684 = (3 + 2 + 9)(6 + 8 + 4) = 1418$

Therefore, $751694 = (7 + 5 + 1)(6 + 9 + 4) = 1319$

Hence, 1319 is the correct answer.

171. The number shall be inserted in such a way that the connected numbers to the given number must have their sum equal to the value given, as

1 – 12
2 – 9
3 – 1
4 – 14
5 – 7
6 – 4

We get the following pattern:

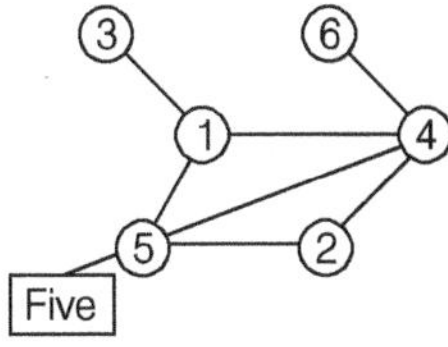

Consider $1 = 3 + 4 + 5 = 12$

$4 = 6 + 2 + 5 + 1 = 14$

$2 = 4 + 5 = 9$

and similarly other numbers satisfy the pattern.

172. The given numbers of animals' cages follow a pattern related to their names where a vowel is counted as 3 and a consonant is counted as 5.

So, we have

Lion $= 5 + 3 + 3 + 5 = 16$

Sea lion $= 5 + 3 + 3 + 5 + 3 + 3 + 5 = 27$

Monkey $= 5 + 3 + 5 + 5 + 5 + 3 = 26$

Antelope $= 3 + 5 + 5 + 3 + 5 + 3 + 5 + 3 = 32$

Buffalo $= 5 + 3 + 5 + 5 + 3 + 5 + 3 = 29$

Hence, the number of Buffalo's cage is 29 .

173. Let four-wheeler be denoted by C and two-wheeler be denoted by S, respectively. Then, the sequence of parking is

C S C S S C S S S C S S S S C S S S/S S C S S S S S S C S S S S S S S C

The above sequence has been divided into two equal halves by a line.

Clearly, the number of two-wheelers in second half of the row is 15.

Note Count only scooter in second half.

174. These are 16 houses between number 12 and number 29. Since, half of those have to be on each side, there are 8 more houses on each side. This makes the last home on one side house number 20 and there must be 20 more homes going back up the street, which makes a total of 40.

Alternate Method

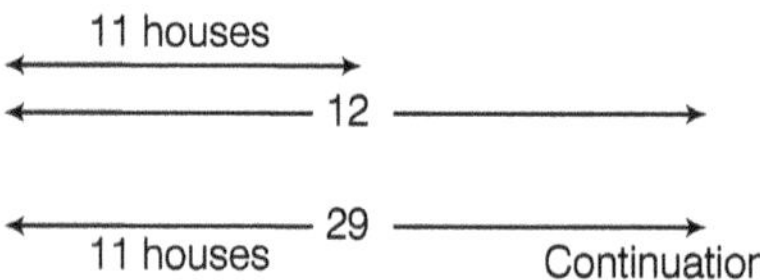

Since, the house on opposite line has number 29. So, there are 29 house as certain, now 29 is opposite to 12 and the sequence will go to 1, so the total number of houses will be $29 + 11 = 40$ houses.

175. On folding the pattern of house, following structures can be formed:

So, only option (c) can be formed by folding the pattern of house.

176.

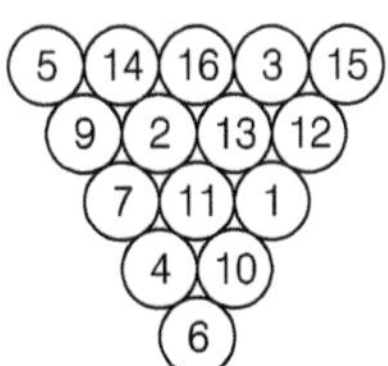

The number on the balls are arranged in the way given in above figure, so that each number is equal to the difference of the number on the two balls above it.

177. Considering all the figures, it is clear that Mathematics wizard number (1) followed the rule, closed figure becoming more and more open and open figure becoming more and more closed in a correct way.

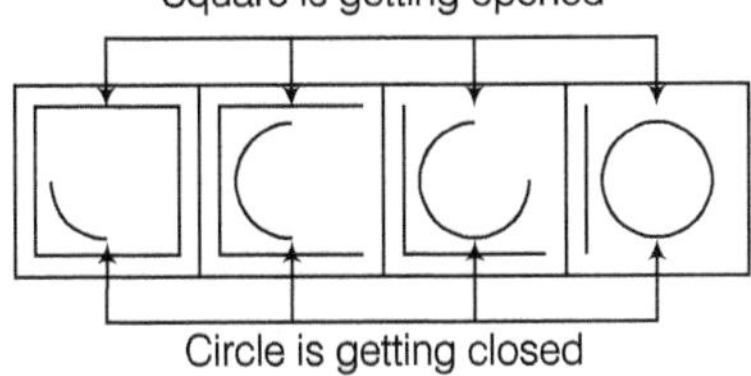

178. The figure may be labelled as shown below:

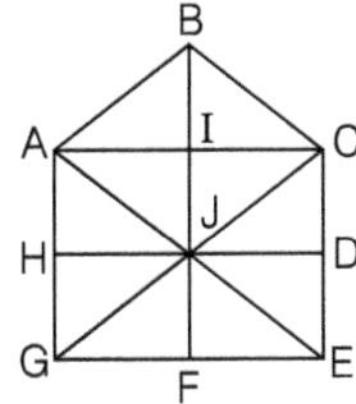

The simplest triangles having one component are ABI, BIC, AIJ, CIJ, AHJ, CDJ, JHG, JDE, GJF and EJF i.e. 10 in number.

The triangles composed of 2 components each are ABC, BCJ, ACJ, BAJ, AJG, CJE and GJE i.e. 7 in number.

The triangle composed of 4 components each are ACG, ACE, CGE and AGE i.e. 4 in number.

$\therefore$ Total number of triangles in the given figure $= 10 + 7 + 4 = 21$

179. The sequence of numbers is as follows:

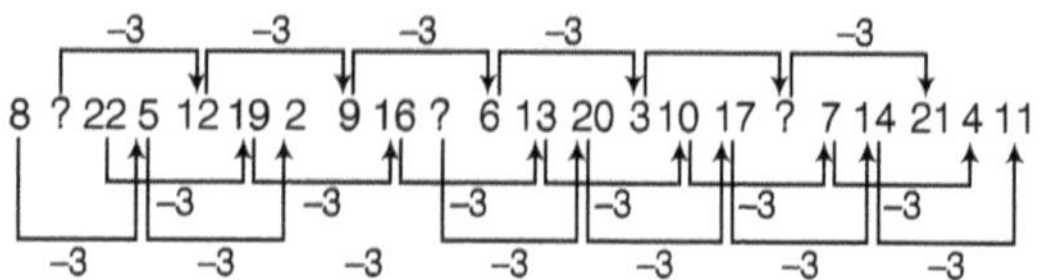

So, first ? $= 12 + 3 = 15$

second ? $= 20 + 3 = 23$

and third ? $= 21 + 3 = 24$

So, the correct circle with sequence is

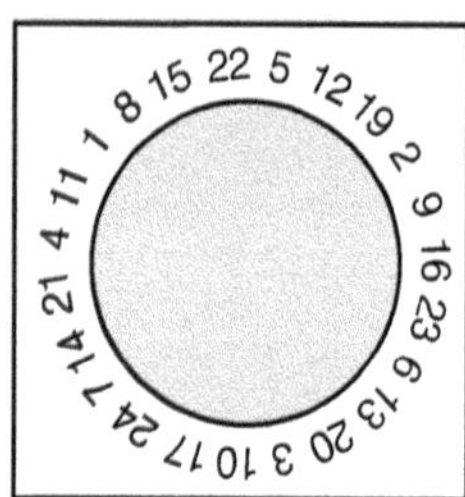

180. The given block is

6		3		5		7		4		8	=	13

The signs to be used are +, −, ÷, ×.

We have,

$6 \times 3 = 18$ and $18 - 5 = 13$

$13 + 7 = 20$

$20 \div 4 = 5$

$5 + 8 = 13$

So, '+' has been used twice and the correct pattern is as follows:

6	×	3	−	5	+	7	÷	4	+	8	=	13

181. Moving clockwise, around alternate segments in the chain, one sequence decreases by 1, 2, 3 and 4 each time, while the other increases by 2, 3, 4 and 5.

Hence, 1st sequence $= 816 - 1 = 815 - 2 = 813 - 3 = 810 - 4 = 806$

and 2nd sequence $= 802 + 2 = 804 + 3 = 807 + 4 = 811 + 5 = 816$

So, the missing number is 816.

182. Normally, newspapers are printed on one large sheet. In a finished section, the first and second pages are printed on half of the sheet, and second to last and last page are on the front and back of the other half. Therefore, the final page of a section of newspaper is usually a multiple of 4. In this case, pages 1 and 2 are attached to 39 and 40 (since, the section contains 40 pages). The rest of the pages are attached like this.

1-2 ↔ 39-40
3-4 ↔ 37-38
5-6 ↔ 35-36
7-8 ↔ 33-34
9-10 ↔ 31-32
11-12 ↔ 29-30
13-<u>14</u> ↔ <u>27-28</u>
15-16 ↔ 25-26
17-18 ↔ 23-24
19-20 ↔ 21-22

Hence, the three missing pages are 14, 27 and 28.

183. The given statements are as follows:

George : Phil broke the glass

Bill : It was not me

Al : It was not Ken

Phil : George is lying

Ken : Bill is telling the truth

Let say George is saying the truth. Then, statement of Bill, Al and Ken are also true which can't be possible as only three statements are true.

Let say Bill, Phil and Ken are telling the truth, this implies that Ken has broken the glass.

184. Let it is x min before 12 noon. Four times as many minutes before 55 min $= x + 4x + 55$

Now, this will be equal to the time 8 am i.e. 4 h before 12 noon.

$\Rightarrow x + 4x + 55 = 4 \times 60$ min

$\Rightarrow \quad 5x + 55 = 240$

$\Rightarrow \quad 5x = 185$

$\Rightarrow \quad x = 37$ min

185. Time shown by the watch $= 6$ pm

Time at which it stopped is 3 h before.

So, the time according to watch $= 9$ pm

Now, the time lost by watch per hour $= 15$ min

So, time lost by watch from 12 noon to 6 pm $= 6 \times \frac{15}{60} = 1.5$ h

$\therefore$ The exact time is 9 pm + 1.5 h = 10:30 pm.

186. Since, Dave spoke to the biologist, and Ann was sitting next to the chemist and across from the doctor, Cathy must be the author, and therefore Ann is the biologist. The doctor did not speak, but Dave did. So, Boobie is the doctor (and was thinking of her own parents) and Dave is the chemist.

187. Let Monika's age be m yr and Barbara's age be b yr.

Now, Barbara is 2 yr younger than Monika.

So, we have $b + 2 = m$

According to the statement that Barbara is not as old as they were together 9 yr ago and Monika is older than they were together 9 yr ago, we have

$$b < (m - a) + (b - a) < b + 2$$

Hence, $(m - a) + (b - a) = b + 1$

$\Rightarrow \quad m = 19$ while $b = m - 2 = 17$

So, Monika is 19 yr old and Barbara is 17 yr old.

188. Number of rounds of single elimination $= 7$

Number of players in each match = 2

$\therefore$ Total number of men's singles players who originally enter when the game begin $= 2^7 = 128$

189. The statements are as follows:

Alan $\rightarrow$ Jack did it.

Jack $\rightarrow$ George did it.

Sid $\rightarrow$ It was not me.

George $\rightarrow$ Jack is lying.

(1) If Alan is guilty, then Sid and George are saying the truth.

(2) If Jack is guilty, then Alan, Sid and George are saying the truth.

(3) If Sid is guilty, then George alone is saying the truth.

(4) If George is guilty, then Jack and Sid are saying the truth.

This implies that Sid is innocent as only one has spoken the truth.

190. Given, area of one tile $= 12$ inch

and number of tiles $= 850$

So, total area of tiles $= 850 \times 12 = 10200$ inch $= 850$ sq ft

Let side of one square floor be x inch. Then, side of other square floor is $(x + 10)$ inch.

According to the problem,

$$x^2 + (x+10)^2 = 850$$

$$\Rightarrow \quad x^2 + x^2 + 100 + 20x = 850$$

$$\Rightarrow \quad 2x^2 + 20x - 750 = 0$$

$$\Rightarrow \quad x^2 + 10x - 375 = 0$$

$$\Rightarrow \quad x^2 + 25x - 15x - 375 = 0$$

$$\Rightarrow \quad x(x+25) - 15(x+25) = 0$$

$$\Rightarrow \quad x = 15, -25$$

So, the side of smaller square is 15 ft and the side of larger square is 25 ft.

191. The middle pattern is shifted to outside and the remaining part of the figure is enclosed inside the middle pattern.

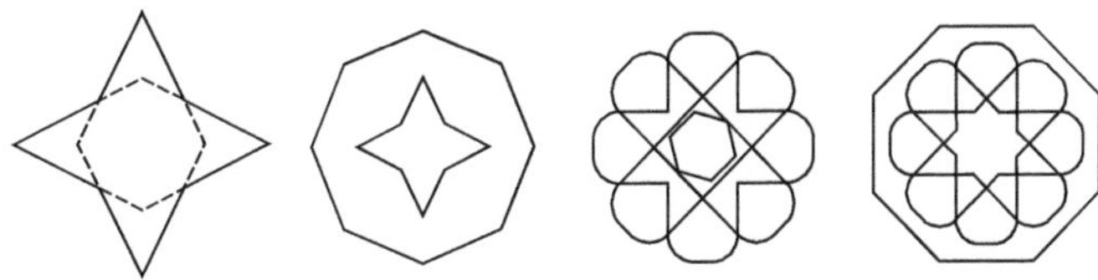

Hence, option (c) is correct.

192. Each of the tile is rotated at an angle of 90° clockwise and moving to the next block in the next figure.

Let the hand is denoted by '↑'.

So,

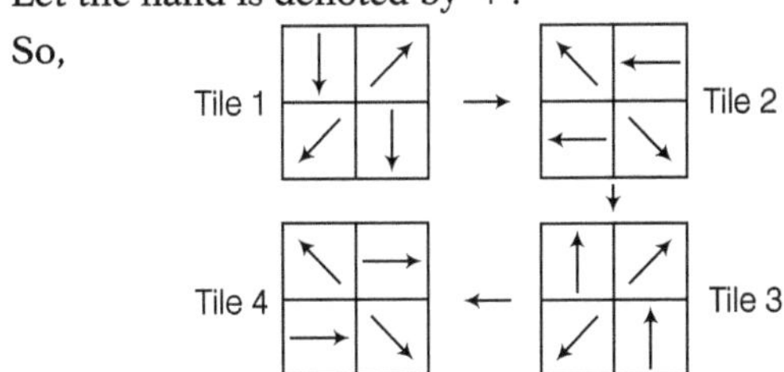

Hence, option (d) is correct.

193. Please note that both numbers must have been at most three-digit ones-otherwise their sum would have had atleast four digits.

We assume that these numbers are abc and def. The sum of $c + f$ must be a number whose last digit is 0, which occurs only for $c = 4$ and $f = 6$ or $c = 6$ and $f = 4$.

Since, $abc + def = 750$ and $c + f = 10$, then $ab + de = 74$.

Therefore, $b + e$ equals 4 or 14, since 14 can't be gained by addition of given numbers. So, $b = 1$ and $e = 3$ or $b = 3$ and $e = 1$.

This means that $a = 2$ and $d = 5$ or $a = 5$ and $d = 2$ (only these two digits have remained).

Hence, the possible pairs of numbers written down by Tom are:

214 and 536, 216 and 534, 234 and 516 or 236 and 514.

194. It is given that, $A = 2$ and $B + P + F = 24$

Now, $A + B = Z$ and $Z + P = T$

$\therefore \quad A + B + P = T \quad \ldots(i)$

Also, $\quad T + A = F$

In the equation,

$$B + P + F = 24$$

$$B + P + T + A = 24$$

$$\Rightarrow \quad B + P + T = 22 \quad [\because A = 2]$$

$$\Rightarrow \quad B + P - 22 = -T \quad \ldots(ii)$$

From Eqs. (i) and (ii), we have

$$B + P + 2 = T$$

$$B + P - 22 = -T$$

$$\underline{- \quad - \quad + \qquad +}$$

$$24 = 2T$$

So, $T = 12$

$\therefore \quad F = T + A = 12 + 2 = 14$

and $\quad Q - T = 7$

$\Rightarrow \quad Q - 12 = 7$

So, $\quad Q = 19$

Now, we know that,

$$F + S = Q$$

$$\Rightarrow \quad 14 + S = 19$$

$$\therefore \quad S = 5$$

Hence, the values of $S = 5$ and $Q = 19$.

195.

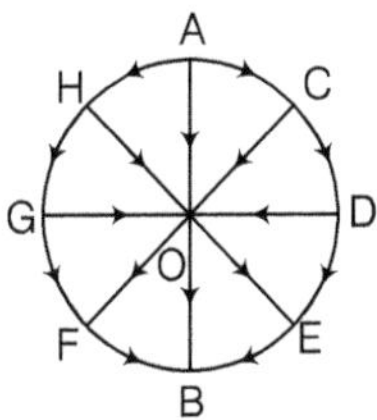

Ways or routes from centre (AO, OB)

(AO, OE, EB)

(AO, OF, FB)

Ways or routes from right side

(AC, CO, OB), (AC,CO, OE, EB),

(AC, CD, DO, OB), (AC, CD, DO, OE, EB)

(AC, CD, DE, EB)

(AC, CO, OF, FB) (AC, CD, DO, OF, FB)

Ways or routes from left side

(AH, HO, OB) (AH, HO, OF, FB)

(AH, HG, GF, FB) (AH, HG, GO, OB)

(AH, HG, GO, OF, FB)

(AH, HO, OE, EB), (AH, HG, GO, OE, EB)

Hence, total 17 routes or ways are there to travel from A to B.

196. Let Tony's age be x yr and Margaret's age be y yr.

According to the question,

$$x^2 + y = 62$$

$$\Rightarrow \quad y = (62 - x^2)$$

and $$y^2 + x = 176$$

We have, $(62 - x^2)^2 + x = 176$

$\Rightarrow 3844 + x^4 - 124x^2 + x = 176$

$\Rightarrow x^4 - 124x^2 + x + 3668 = 0$

Let $x = 7$, then we have LHS

$$(7)^4 - 124(7)^2 + (7) + 3668$$

$$= 2401 - 6076 + 7 + 3668$$

$$= 6076 - 6076 = 0$$

$\therefore \quad x = 7$ [correct]

Now, $y = 62 - 7^2 = 62 - 49 = 13$

Hence, Tony's age is 7 yr and Margaret's age is 13 yr.

197. Since, the number of cheese pieces are 4 and the stools are 2.

∴ Number of moves required to move these pieces to stool C

$$= 2^4 - 1 = 16 - 1 = 15$$

198. If we assume the length of side of one of the smaller squares be x, then the length of side of other square is $3x$.

∴ Area of the two smaller squares $= x^2 + (3x)^2 = x^2 + 9x^2$

Also, area of these two smaller squares is equal to the area of one large square (490 sq ft).

$$\therefore \quad x^2 + 9x^2 = 490$$

$$\Rightarrow \quad 10x^2 = 490$$

$$\Rightarrow \quad x = 7$$

$$\therefore \quad 3x = 7 \times 3 = 21$$

So, the area of one square $= x^2 = 49$ sq ft

and the area of other square $= 9x^2 = 441$ sq ft

199. According to the given statements, number '7' satisfies the conditions as

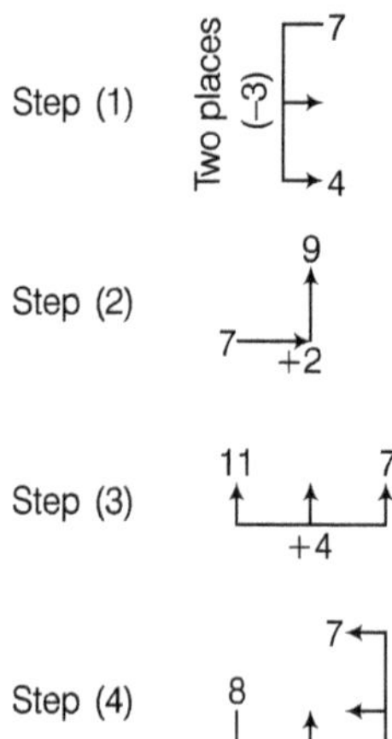

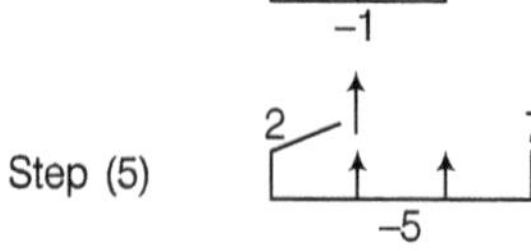

200. The correct arrangement of numbers, to have a total of 14 of the three numbers, is as follows:

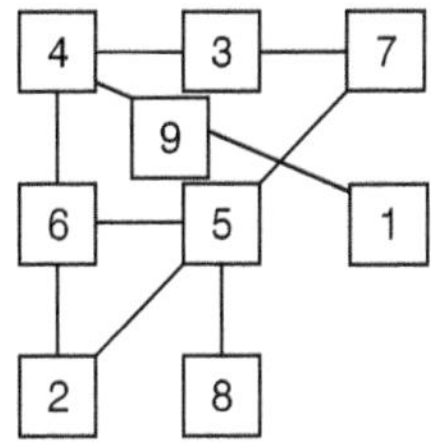

201. As per the information,

$$\text{Al} + \text{Bob} = 150 \quad \text{...(i)}$$

$$\text{Bob} + \text{Cal} = 200 \quad \text{...(ii)}$$

$$\text{Cal} + \text{Dot} = 170 \quad \text{...(iii)}$$

$$\text{Dot} + \text{Ed} = 210 \quad \text{...(iv)}$$

$$\text{Ed} + \text{Al} = 100 \quad \text{...(v)}$$

In order to find the amount each one paid, we are required to solve the above equations.

From Eqs. (i) and (v), we get

$$\text{Bob} - \text{Ed} = 50 \quad \text{...(vi)}$$

and $\text{Bob} - \text{Dot} = 30$ [from Eqs. (ii) and (iii)] ...(vii)

We have,

$\text{Dot} - \text{Ed} = 20$ [from Eqs. (vi) and (vii)] ...(viii)

From Eqs. (iv) and (viii), we get

$$2\ \text{Dot} = 230$$

$\Rightarrow$ Dot = ₹ 115

and Cal = ₹ 55

$\therefore$ Ed = ₹ 95

Bob = ₹ 145

Al = ₹ 5

So, the money spent by Al is ₹ 5, Bob is ₹ 145, Cal is ₹ 55, Dot is ₹ 115 and Ed is ₹ 95.

202. We know that,

$$BBB = B \times 111$$

Now, $111 = 3 \times 37$

So, $BBB = B \times 3 \times 37$

This means the right side is divisible by 37 and 3. Therefore, the left side must also be divisible by 37 and 3.

Since, 37 is a prime number, so the left side is to be divisible by 37 must have a two-digit multiple of 37. (as $AB \times A \times B = BBB$)

Now, $AB \times A \times B = BBB$

So, $AB = 37$ or 74

$\Rightarrow$ $A = 3$ or 7 and $B = 7$ or 4

Consider each case for $A = 7$ and $B = 4$

$AB \times A \times B = 74 \times 7 \times 4$, but is not divisible by 3. So, we will consider $AB = 37$ such that $37 \times 3 \times 7 = 777 = 7 \times 111$.

$\therefore$ $A = 3$ and $B = 7$ are the correct values.

203. The number of people standing in queue are 7 namely A, B, C, D, E, F and G.

Statement 1 Number of people standing infront of A is same as the number of people standing behind C.

↑
A
C
↓

Statement 2 Three people are standing between B and F. So, we have

B
____
____
____
F

Statement 3 B is standing behind A. So, we have

A
B
____
____
____
F

Since, 5 people are already being placed, so no one stands before A and therefore, behind C.

A
B
____
____
____
F
C

Statement 4 Number of people standing infront of G is same as the number standing behind D.

The following cases arise:

A
B

D
G
F
C

But the condition is not satisfied.

A
B
D
G

F
C

In this case, also the condition is not satisfied.

So, the correct position will be

1 — A
2 — B
3 — G/D
4 — E
5 — D/G
6 — F
7 — C

204. Number of rows are two.

Statement 1 Six persons in each row.

Persons sitting in row 1 are A, B, C, D, E and F and persons sitting in row 2 are P, Q, R, S, T and V.

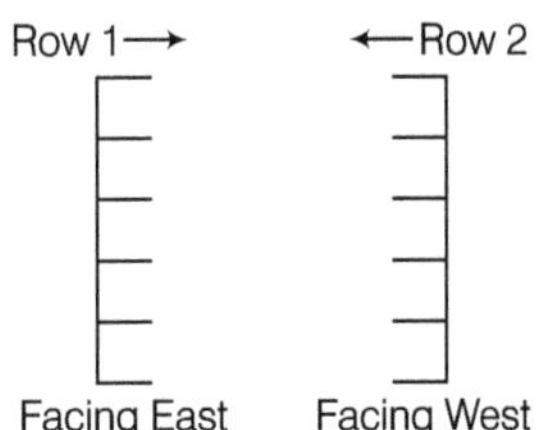

P is sitting at one of the ends of the row is second to the right of T.

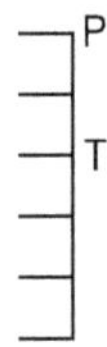

Statement 2 A does not face P or T.

Statement 3 A is third to the left of F.

Statement 4 C and D do not face P and B is neighbour of C.

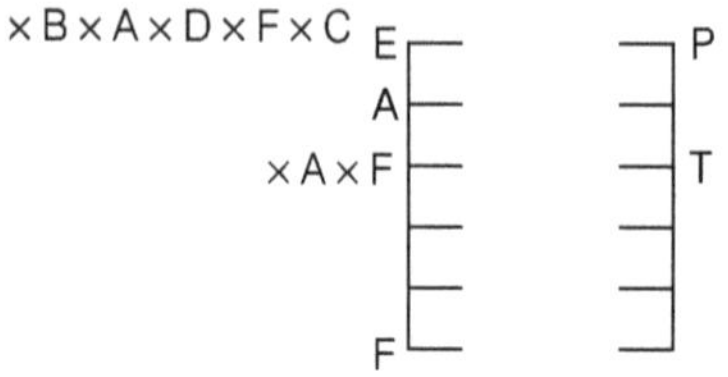

×B×A×D×F×C E — — P

A — —

×A×F — — T

F — —

Statement 5 There is only one person between C and D and B is neighbour of C. So,

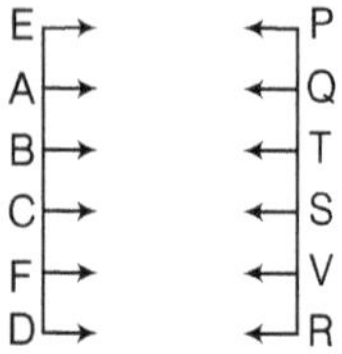

E →		← P
A →		← Q
B →		← T
C →		← S
F →		← V
D →		← R

Statement 6 There are two persons between Q and V and S, who doesn't face D, is not the neighbour of Q.

So, the number of people sitting between E and C are two namely A and B.

205. Consider $A^1 = 2^5$

and $B^1 = 2^4 + 2^3 + 2^2 + 2^1$

Now, $A^1 = 2^5 = 32$

and $B^1 = 2^4 + 2^3 + 2^2 + 2^1 + 2^0$

$= 16 + 8 + 4 + 2 + 1 = 31$

So, $A^1 > B^1$ and $A^1 = B^1 + 1$

Let $A^{11} = 2^6$

and $B^{11} = 2^5 + 2^4 + 2^3 + 2^2 + 2^1 + 2^0$

So, $A^{11} = 64$

and $B^{11} = 32 + 16 + 8 + 4 + 2 + 1 = 63$

$\Rightarrow A^{11} > B^{11}$ and $A^{11} = B^{11} + 1$

For any power of 2 (2^n),

If $A_0 = 2^n$ and $B_0 = 2^{n-1} + 2^{n-2} + \ldots + 2^0$,

then $A_0 > B_0$

So, $A(= 2^{65}) > B(= 2^{64} + 2^{63} + \ldots + 2^0)$

Hence, A is larger than B by 1.

206. There can be different cases to answer this puzzle depending on the answer of his friend which are as follows:

I. Question 1: Yes, 1-40
Question 2: Yes, 8, 12, 20, 24, 28, 32, 40
Question 3: No
But, it is not possible to answer in this case.

II. Question 1: Yes, 1-40
Question 2: No,
Question 3: Yes, 9, 25
Still, we can't find an absolute answer.

III. Question 1: No, 42-82
Question 2: Yes, 44-48-52-56-60, 64, 68, 72, 76, 80
Question 3: Yes, 64

Hence, 64 is the correct answer which is the house number of his friend.

207. The statements can be inferred as follows:

1. All but four are brown means all are brown except four.
2. All but four are blue means all are blue except four.
3. All but four are grey means all are grey except four.
4. All but four are green means all are green except four.
5. All but four are black means all are black except four.

All of the above statements means there are only five jackets each of colour blue, grey, green, brown and black.

208. Hanralty's = Dutchman + 2

Edna = Sal – 6

Sal = Hanralty's + 2

Dutchman = Edna + 2

Sal > Hanralty > Dutchman > Edna
–2 –2 –2

Total number of cases = 20

i.e. Hanralty + Dutchman + Edna + Sal = 20

$\Rightarrow$ Dutchman + 2 + Dutchman + Dutchman – 2 + Sal = 20

$\Rightarrow$ 3 Dutchman + Sal = 20

$\Rightarrow$ 3 Dutchman + Hanralty + 2 = 20

$\Rightarrow$ 3 Dutchman + Dutchman + 2 + 2 = 20

$\Rightarrow$ 4 Dutchman = 16 and Dutchman received 4 cases.

$\therefore$ Edna received 2 cases, Hanralty received 6 cases and Sal received 8 cases.

209. The finance company was adding and subtracting 10% of a term to obtain the next term of the series.

Therefore, 10000 + (10% of 10000) = 11000 (in 2nd month)

11000 – (10% of 11000) = 9900 (in 3rd month)

9900 + (10% of 9900) = 10890 (in 4th month)

10890 – (10% of 10890) = 9801 (in 5th month)

9801 + (10% of 9801) = 9801 + 980 = 10781 (in 6th month)

So, the villagers would just receive ₹ 10781 in 6th month.

210. Number of dishes are 6 namely A, B, C, D, E and F.

Statement 1 A is adjacent to F and A is opposite to desserts which is not B.

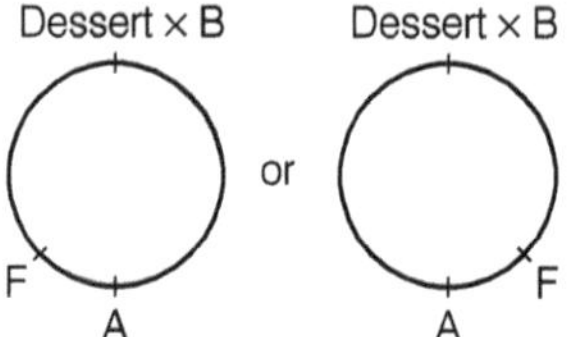

Statement 2 C is not adjacent to either B or E.

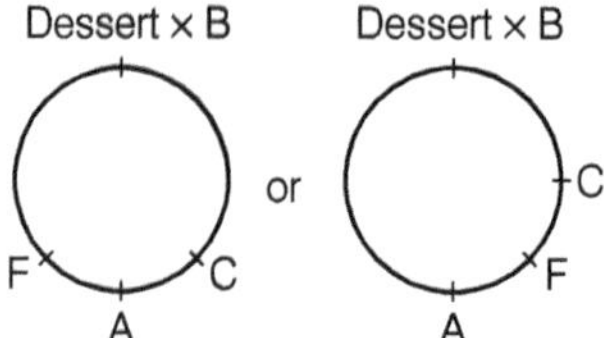

Statement 3 D is the main course and is adjacent to desserts.

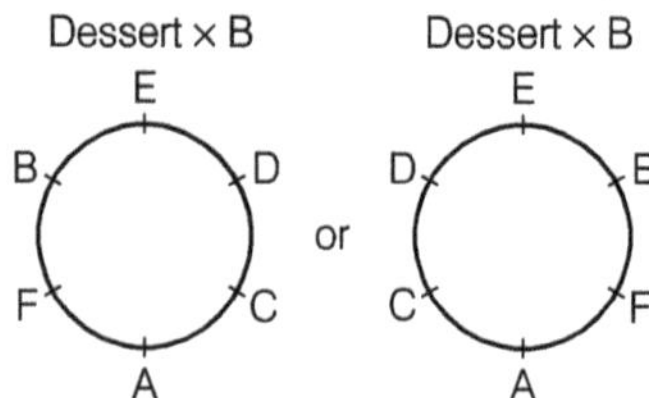

So, the arrangement is as follows:

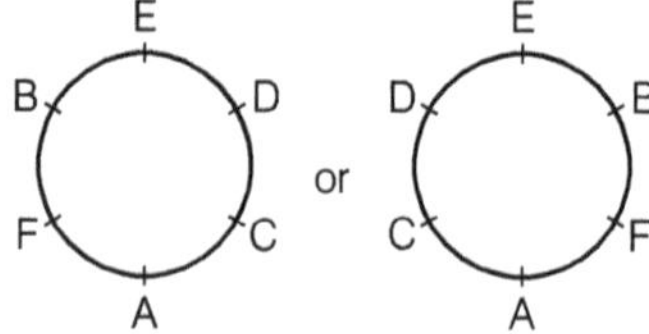

Hence, it is clear from the arrangement that dish A is opposite to E.

211. The numerical logic to crack the number sequence is as follows:

Start from the number 4 moving anti-clockwise in spiral way by first adding 2 and then subtracting 1.

i.e. 4 (+ 2) 6 (− 1) 5 (+ 2) 7 (− 1) 6 (+ 2) 8 (− 1) 7 (+ 2) 9 (− 1) 8 (+ 2) 10 and so on.

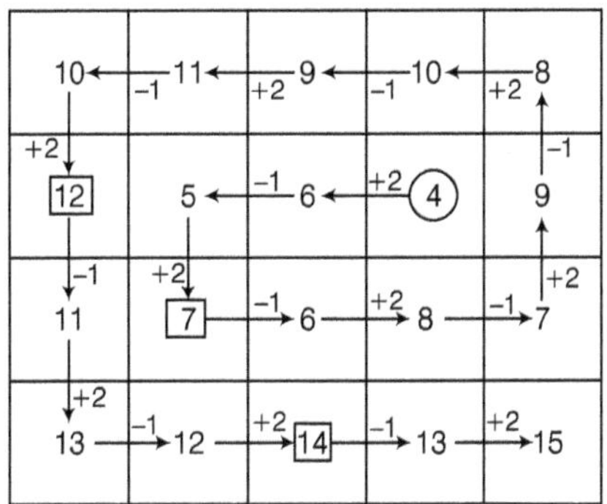

212. There are 300 min between 2:00 and 7:00 and we can ignore the '40 min ago' for a little while and share the remaining 260 min in the ratio 3 : 1, which is 195 : 65.

Which means the 5 h between 2:00 and 7:00 are made up of 195 min + 40 min + 65 min.

Which means it is currently 65 min before 7:00. So, it is now 5:55 (65 min before 7:00).

To double check, 40 min ago it was 5:15, which is 195 min after 2:00, as required (as $65 \times 3 = 195$).

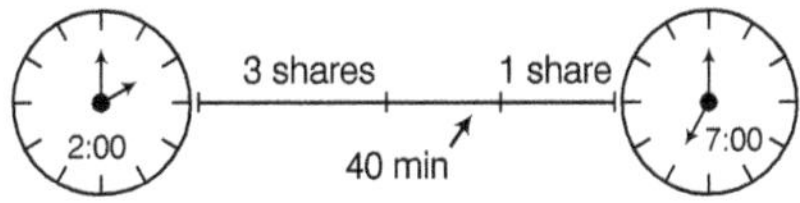

Hence, the required answer is 65 min.

213. **Statement 1** Number below 500 means 1 to 499.

Statement 2 Square number means 4, 9, 25, 36, 49, 69, 81, 100, 121, 169, 196, 225, 256, 289, 324, 361, 400, 441, 484

Statement 3 It is a cube number 64.

Statement 4 The first and last digits are 5, 7 or 9.

So, all the conditions do not match up.

∴ Statement 1 is a lie as the numbers which are perfect square and cube both are 64 and 729.

So, the required answer is 729.

214. In the first lot,

1 tractor + 3 shovels + 7 trucks = ₹ 140

In the second lot,

1 tractor + 4 shovels + 10 trucks = ₹ 170

In the third lot,

1 tractor + 1 shovel + 5 trucks = ₹ 100

From first and second lots,

1 shovel + 3 trucks = 30

and from third and second lots,

3 shovel + 5 trucks = 70

So, we have

3 shovel + 9 trucks = 90

3 shovel + 5 trucks = 70

⇒ 4 trucks = ₹ 20

⇒ 1 truck = ₹ 5

∴ 1 shovel = 30 − 15 = ₹ 15 and 1 tractor = 140 − 45 − 35 = ₹ 60

Therefore, the amount paid for lot number fourth

$= 10 \times 60 + 15 \times 15 + 25 \times 5 = 600 + 225 + 125 =$ ₹ 950

and amount paid for lot number fifth

$= 1 \times 60 + 1 \times 15 + 1 \times 5 = 60 + 15 + 5 =$ ₹ 80

215. ○○○ = LAG RAB = ○ ○ (vertical)

◇◇ = LEB

REG = ◇ ◇ ◇ (vertical)

1. The equations with horizontal arrangement includes L and the figures with vertical arrangement includes R.
2. The equations with '○' includes A and the figures with '◇' includes E.
3. The equations having three figures includes G and the equations having two figures include B.

Therefore,

◇◇◇ = LEG

and REBRAG = ◇ ◇ ○ ○ ○ (vertical)

216. Cost of one cream cake = Cost of two fruit cakes

= Cost of three doughnuts = ₹1

∴ Cost of one cream cake + Cost of one fruit cake + Cost of 1 doughnut

$$= 1 + \frac{1}{2} + \frac{1}{3} = \frac{6+3+2}{6} = \frac{₹11}{6}$$

Now, total money given by the parents is ₹ 11 and cost of one set of three cakes is ₹ $\frac{11}{6}$, therefore 6 such sets of three cakes are bought by Jeremy and his brother Roger.

Now, each kid got same number of same cakes, therefore 6 sets of three cakes can be distributed among one, two, three or six kids.

Now, there are already two boys Jeremy and Rogery and the number of girls are same as number of boys, so there are atleast two girls. Therefore, there are minimum 4 kids. Now, number of kids can one, two, three or six.

So, the total number of kids are six (three boys and three girls).

217. By using simple addition, the diagonals of the figure can be filled in the following manner such that the sum of the numbers in each diagonal is same and one of the numbers from 1 to 9 is included in each diagonal at the intersection point.

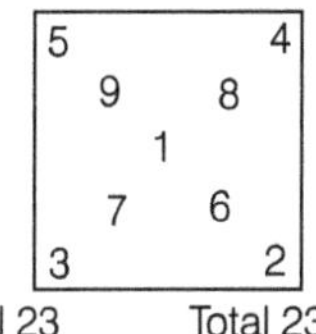

218. **Statement 1** Two places between Florence and Ernie and Ernie was immediately infront of Andrea.

Ernie
Andrea
_____
_____
Florence

or

Florence
_____
_____
Ernie
Andrea

Statement 2 Celia was three places infront of Daniel.

Celia
_____
_____
Daniel

Statement 3 Gertie was immediately infront of Henry.

Gertie
Henry

Statement 4 Brian is somewhere infront of Florence.

Statement 5 Henry was somewhere infront of Celia.

Statement 6 There were two places between Andrea and Brian.

So, we get the arrangement as

1. Gertie
2. Henry
3. Brian
4. Celia
5. Ernie
6. Andrea
7. Daniel
8. Florence

So, Dopey's pseudonym was Celia.

219. The middle number at the bottom is the result of the addition of two side numbers less the top middle number, as follows:

$4 + 6 = 10 - 3 = 7$

$3 + 3 = 6 - 3 = 3$

$7 + 2 = 9 - 4 = 5$

So, $? = 7 + 5 - 3 = 12 - 3 = \boxed{9}$

220. In each of the section, the dot is included in two shapes either between a circle and a triangle or between a triangle or square or between a circle and square, but in option (d) the dot is in all the 3 shapes, which makes it the odd one among others.

Hence, option (d) is correct.

221. In the given figure, at the top the triangle overlaps the bigger circle and a right angled line runs parallel to the whole of one side of the triangle.

Therefore in option (d), we can add the small circle which will satisfy the same condition as in the figure given above.

Hence, option (d) is correct.

222. Surveen runs 2000 m while Jasmin run 1970 m and Japneet runs 1900 m.

At the same rate, Jasmin runs 1500 m whilst Japneet runs

$$\frac{2000 \times 1900}{1970} = 1928.93 \text{ m}$$

Hence, Jasmin beats Japneet by 71.06 m.

223. The sum of the numbers on the four corners of the first square is equal to the number in the centre of second square.

Now, the sum of the numbers on the four corners of the third square $= 2 + 4 + 8 + 11 = 25$.

Also, the sum of the two consecutive numbers on the corner of the first square is equal to the number on the second square.

$$5 + 3 = 8$$
$$3 + 4 = 7$$
$$4 + 9 = 13$$
$$5 + 9 = 14$$

From the third square,

$$2 + 4 = 6$$
$$4 + 8 = 12$$
$$8 + 11 = 19$$
$$11 + 2 = 13$$

So, the fourth square will be

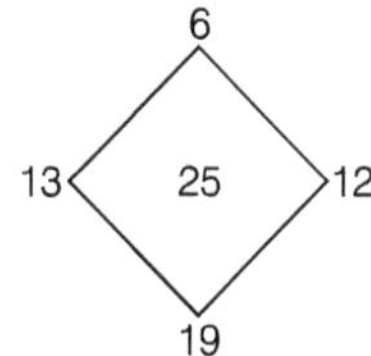

Hence, option (a) is correct.

224. Since, the plus and minus signs are decreased to only three so the digits will be combined to form a two or three digit numbers as follows:

$$123 - 45 - 67 + 89 = 100$$

225. Let's have a look at the number of watermelons just before the appearance of the last buyer. If Ms. Cindy had bought only half of the remaining watermelons, Catherine would have been left with a melon and a half. So, Catherine had 3 watermelons before Ms. Cindy arrived.

Similarly, before Ms. Barbara's arrival, she had $2 \times (3 + 0.5) = 7$ watermelons, and before Ms. Angela showed up, she had $2 \times (7 + 0.5) = 15$ watermelons. Catherine sold then 14 melons, earning $14 \times 2 = \$\ 28$.

So, Catherine's takings amounted to $ 28.

www.ingramcontent.com/pod-product-compliance
Ingram Content Group UK Ltd.
Pitfield, Milton Keynes, MK11 3LW, UK
UKHW021659190726
13853UKWH00001B/352